Abstracts of Alleghany County Virginia DEEDS

1822–1829

Marsha Martin

HERITAGE BOOKS
2013

HERITAGE BOOKS
AN IMPRINT OF HERITAGE BOOKS, INC.

Books, CDs, and more—Worldwide

For our listing of thousands of titles see our website at
www.HeritageBooks.com

Published 2013 by
HERITAGE BOOKS, INC.
Publishing Division
100 Railroad Ave. #104
Westminster, Maryland 21157

Originally published 1997

Other Heritage Books by Marsha Martin:

Abstracts of Alleghany County, Virginia Deeds, 1822–1829

Abstracts of Alleghany County, Virginia Deeds, 1829–1833

Lancaster County, Pennsylvania Land Records, 1729–1750 and Land Warrants, 1710–1742

All rights reserved. No part of this book may be reproduced or transmitted in any form or by any means, electronic or mechanical, including photocopying, recording or by any information storage and retrieval system without written permission from the author, except for the inclusion of brief quotations in a review.

International Standard Book Numbers
Paperbound: 978-1-58549-430-9
Clothbound: 978-0-7884-6924-4

CONTENTS

Introduction v

Explanation of Some Legal Terms vii

Maps
    Town of Covington x
    City of Covington - 1890 xi

Deed Book 1 1

Index 87

INTRODUCTION

Alleghany County was created from Botetourt County, Bath County, and Monroe County. The beginning of the settlement in Alleghany was in Augusta County until 1769. From 1769 to 1789 it was in Botetourt County. In 1790, part was in Bath County, Monroe County, and some still in Botetourt County. Early records can be found in Fincastle, Staunton, and Warm Springs. Although the county name is spelled different, it did receive its name from its location at the base of the Allegheny Mountains.

The earliest recorded settlers in Alleghany were Jacob Persinger, Peter Wright, and Joseph Carpenter. In 1750, Peter Wright recorded a survey of 286 acres covering most of the area of Covington, which is now the county seat. Dr. James Merry and his brother Samuel became the owners of the Wright farm and a small cluster of houses which became known as Merry's Store. In 1819, Covington was designated as a town. There are two stories surrounding the name of Covington. One story states that the town was named after Peter Covington, who was the oldest resident at the time. The other story is that it was named after General Leonard Covington who was a hero of the War of 1812. The county of Alleghany was formed in 1822 and the city of Covington was first incorporated in 1833.

In Alleghany County in 1822, there were 534 men liable for poll tax. In 1830, there were 2,816 persons listed in the census. In 1843, there were 13 school houses, by 1850 there were eight schools, and eight teachers with 153 pupils. In 1855, there were 43 houses in Covington on two streets. Today's population is at 27,820.

Included in this book are two maps. The first is the original layout of Covington found in the deed book. The description is on 1:340. The second was received from the Alleghany Highlands Genealogical Society, Inc. It gives a better idea of the changes that took place when the Chesapeake and Ohio railroad came through. The names of the streets were changed in early 1953. This change was due to the annexation of the Town of Covington to become a city of the second class.

The sources I used in abstracting the deeds were LDS film #0030512, books 1-3 covering the years 1822 -1839, and LDS film #1888420, books 1-2. The latter is a second filming and a much clearer copy. These films are of the original records at the Alleghany County Courthouse in Covington. Permission to use the films was received from Conley Edwards, Archivist for the Library of Virginia, and Michael D. Wolfe, Clerk of Alleghany County.

The formatused in this volume is as follows: the first number is the deed book, second number is the page number. Next the date of the indenture, followed by the name or names of the Grantor and his county of residence. Then the name of the Grantee and his county of residence. (If a county is not mentioned, they are from Alleghany County.) Next comes the amount paid for the land and then the number of acres, followed by a description and neighbors if mentioned. Then the signatures, witness, acknowledgment, release of dower, and last the date the deed was recorded in Alleghany County. The order of information may vary a little depending on the amount of information included in the deed. Where there is a ?, the print was either unreadable or many times in the fold of the page. Where there is a _ (blank space), it was blank in the deed. For a copy of the entire record you can refer to the LDS films, which can be ordered at your local Family History Center. In addition, you may write to the Alleghany Highlands Genealogical Society, Inc., Room 102 Rivermont School, Rockbridge Street, Covington, VA 24426, or the County Clerk Office, P. O. Box 670, Covington, VA 24426.

Land records are probably one of the best sources of information for the family researcher or the professional genealogist. They can contain a wealth of information. Many early settlers owned land. The most sought after title to the land was called Fee Simple, which meant that the land would desccend to one's heirs if one died without a will. Land could also be devised by a will or sale by the owner. You can find relationships and names of family members in deeds, not only of immediate family, such as wives, but sometimes also grandchildren. It is not usual to find information on related families. (These names are not often included in the index.) Deeds also state the place of residence. Often a person would move before selling his land. When it was sold, it was recorded in the County where the land was located and listed the person's new place of residence. Often neighbors are listed in deeds. This can be very important, as so many of the early settlers married their neighbors. Their value to the genealogist can not be overstated.

On the following pages are a brief explanation of some of the terms you may encounter in reading these abstracts.

EXPLANATION OF SOME LEGAL TERMS

ADMINISTRATOR - Person who is appointed by the court to settle an estate. He must give security.

ACKNOWLEDGMENT - (ack'd) A formal statement at the end of the deed where an authorized official certifies that the person who executed the deed also signed it of his own free will. Sometimes the term certified (cert'd) is used instead or along with, it means the same.

BOND - An interest-bearing certificate of debt, obligating the issuer to pay the principal at a specified time. To put a certified debt upon, to furnish bond for; be surety for someone.

CAVEAT - Instrument filed by interested party stopping the process of obtaining a grant until the courts decide if the land is actually unappropriated and eligible for patenting. A caution or warning by an interested party to avoid misinterpretation.

CREDITOR - One to whom money, goods, or services is owed.

COVERT - To assume possession of illegally.

DEBTOR - One who owes money, goods or services to another.

DEED - The document by which title in real property is transferred from one party to another. The sale of a Land Grant, recorded in County Clerks Office.

DEVISEE - The person to whom property is devised by a will.

DEVISOR - The person who distributes property through a will.

ESTATE - The total of a persons possessions and property.

ENTRY - The county surveyor's recording of an applicant's intention to file for a patent. The type of warrant being used, the acreage, and the approximate location of the land to be appropriated is included.

EXECUTOR - The person named in the will, by the deceased, to see that all the provisions are carried out.

GIFT DEED - A deed in which real property is transferred without normal consideration. Usually such deeds transfer land from a parent to his child.

GRANT - Document issued by the governor finalizing the patenting process. The original is sent to the recipient of the land and a copy is entered in the Land Office Grant Books.

GRANTEE - The recipient of a grant.

GRANTOR - The person by whom a grant is made.

GUARDIAN - The person appointed to manage the responsibility of the rights and property of another, usually a child.

INDENTURE - The conveyance of a deed.

INTESTATE - A person who dies without making a will, or if for some reason the will is not valid.

LAND MEASURE - 1 mile = 80 chains, 320 rods, 1,760 yard or 5,280feet - 16 1/2 feet = 1 rod or pole - 1 chain = 66 feet or 4 rods - 160 rods = 1 acre - 640 acres = 1 square mile.

MILITARY WARRANT - Document given to soldiers as payment for military service. It authorized the patenting of unappropriated land. The size of the land allotment was determined by the soldier's rank. The soldier could assign the warrant to another party in exchange for money or other goods.

PARTITION - The division of real property among heirs.

PATENT - Method of appropriating vacant land owned by the Commonwealth. Patents consist of three progressions; Warrant, Survey, and Grant.

PLAT - Surveyor's drawing of the tract to be patented.

POWER OF ATTORNEY - The document by which a person appoints another to act for him in a certain matter.

RELEASE - This is a document in which a person gives up his right to another to land in which he has a just claim. This is usually done by the heir to property that is yet undivided.

RELEASE OF DOWER - A document by which the widow relinquishes all claims to her husbands estate. It is important for the purchaser to receive this document, because without it the the widow can come back as many as fifty years after the sale and legally claim her dower rights in the land.

SURVEY - To determine accurately the area, contour, or boundaries of land by measuring lines and angles.

QUIT-RENT - An established rent paid yearly to the crown allowing the homesteader to use the land without direct ownership.

TREASURY WARRANT - Document purchased from the land office authorizing a survey to be made.

TRUST - The confidence, reposed in a person to whom the legal title to property is conveyed for the benefit of another.

TRUSTEE - One who holds property in trust and is charged with carrying out the terms of the indenture.

TRUST DEED - The act of placing the title to real property in one or more trustees to secure the payment of a debt. This arrangement allows the property to be sold in case of a default.

WARRANT - The first step in obtaining a land patent, this document authorizes a survey to be made. It does not stipulate where the land is to be located, only the size of the tract allotted. Types of warrants: Military, Treasury, Proclamation, Settlement Certificate, Preemption, Importation, and Exchange.

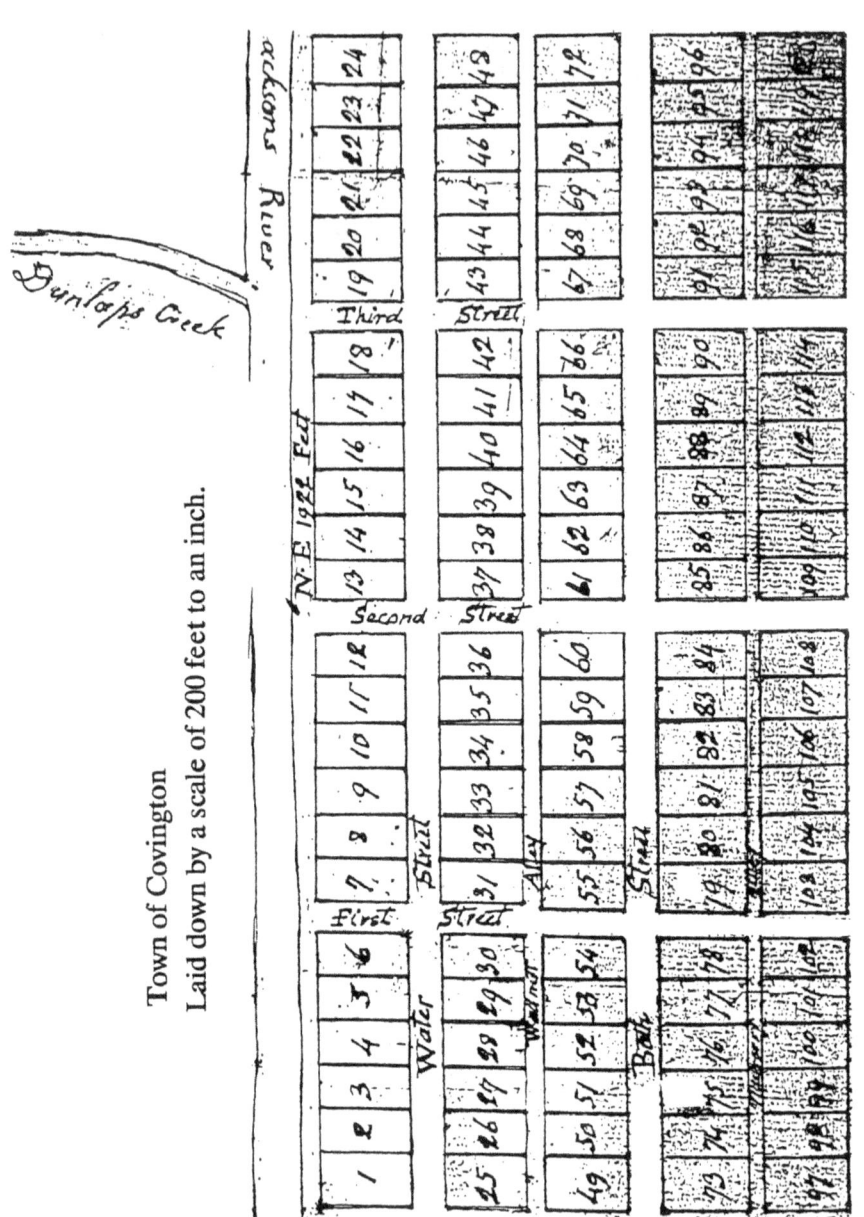

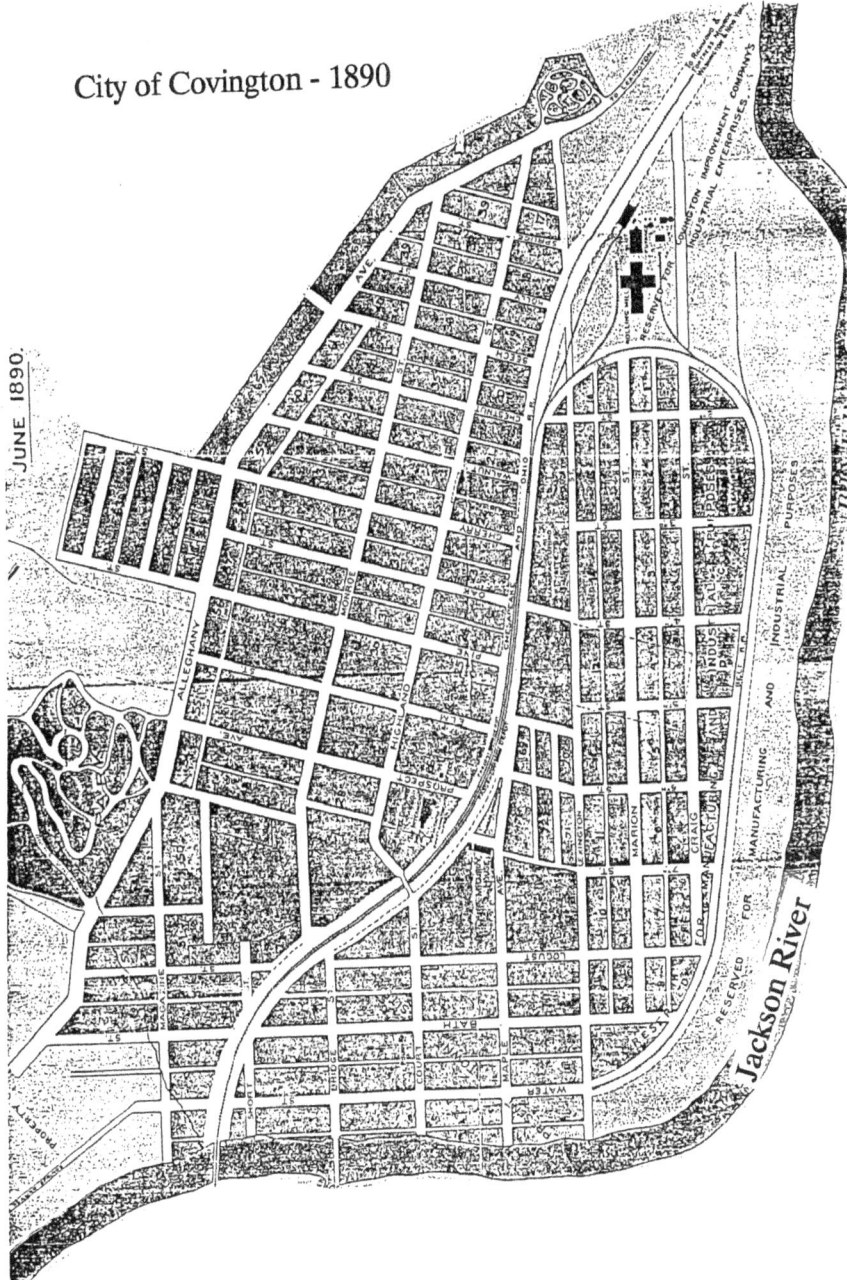

City of Covington - 1890

ALLEGHANY COUNTY, VIRGINIA
Deed Book 1

Know all men by these presents that we William Herbert, Moses Mann Sr., Moses Mann Jr., Samuel Brown, Isaac Johnston, Andrew Sawyer, John Callaghan, and James Merry are held and firmly bound unto Thomas M. Randalph Esquire governor of the Commonwealth of Virginia and his successors for the use of the Commonwealth in the just and full term of $30,000, the payment where of will and truly to be made to our said governor or his successor for the time being we do and ourselves our heirs executors and administrators jointly and severally firmly by these presents sealed with our seals and dated this 18th day of Mar 1822.

The condition of the above obligation is such that whereas the above bound William Herbert is constituted and appointed Sheriff of the County of Allehgany by a commission from the governor under the seal of the Commonwealth bearing date 30 Jan 1822. If, therefore, the said William Herbert shall were and truly collect all levies and poor rates and account for the pay the same in such manner as is by law directed and also all fines forfeitures and assessments occurring or becoming due to the Commonwealth in the said country and shall duly account and pay the same to the treasurer of the Commonwealth for the time being for the use of the Commonwealth in like manner as is or shall be in case of public taxes and shall in all other things truly and faithfully execute the said office of Sheriff during his continuance therein then this obligation to be void else to remain in full force and virtue.....Signed and acknowledged in open court - William Herbert, Moses Mann, Moses H. Mann, Samuel Brown, Andrew Sawyer, Isaac Johnson, John Callaghan, James Merry...This bond was executed and acknowledged in open court by the obligers and the same is ordered to be recorded...Teste Oliver Callaghan.

1:5 - THIS INDENTURE - 6 Sept 1822 - Jacob Butcher Sr., Nancy wife of Fairfield Co. OH to James Merry of Alleghany Co. James Merry paid $200 for 100A located on north side of Jackson River. Bordering land purchased by Merry from Armentrout, sold by Butcher to William Hill...Jacob (X) Butcher... witness - W. Mallow (in dutch),

William Dressler, Isaac Steel...Rec'd Sept 1822 - Oliver Callaghan. Lifted by Maj. Robert Kelso 16 Oct 1828.

18 May 1822 - Andrew Hamilton appointed clerk of Superior Court of Alleghany, bond - $10,000 by John G. Griffin, J. C. Madison, Jacob Neece, Jacob Rudisill, William A. McDowell. Witness - James Woodville, T. B. Miller. Rec'd 20 May 1822 Oliver Callaghan

1:6 19 Aug 1822 - William Herbert appointed Sheriff of Alleghany Co. bond - $30,000 by Moses H. Mann, Samuel Brown, James Merry, Andrew Sawyers, John Crow. Rec'd Aug 1822 Oliver Callaghan.

1:8 15 Jul 1822 - Oliver Callaghan appointed clerk of Alleghany Co. bond - $600 by John Callaghan. Rec'd Jul 1822 Oliver Callaghan.

1:9 - 17 Jun 1822 - William Herbert appointed Surveyor of Alleghany Co., bond $3,000 - Charles Callaghan, William Herbert, Jacob Persinger. Rec'd Jun 1822 Oliver Callaghan.

16 Sept 1822 - William Holloway appointed commissioner of the Public Revenue of Alleghany Co., bond - $1,000 by William H. Haynes, John Holloway. Rec'd Sept 1822 Oliver Callaghan.

1:10 - THIS INDENTURE - 22 Sept 1821 - between Leonard Buzzard, Hannah wife of Greenbrier Co. to Francis Foster of Bath Co., $1 for 3 tracts containing 46A in Bath Co. on Jackson River. Neighbors - Barnard Pitzer, and Sprowl's heirs...Leonard (X) Buzzard, Hannah (X) Buzzard... Release of dower in Bath Co. by justices of the peace, Robert Kincade and Alex McClintic.

1:12 - THIS INDENTURE - 1 May 1822 - William Callaghan of Alleghany to John Callaghan of same, $5, for one 10th part of sale of father, D. Callaghan's estate, land and personal property. Located on Oglies Creek 717A - 28A of which father deeded to Christopher Baughman. neighbors - Brown, David Robinson, McCallisters...William Callaghan...Rec'd 25 May 1822 Oliver Callaghan. Lifted by John Callaghan 19 Mar 1838.

1:13 - THIS INDENTURE - Benjamin Haynes of Alleghany gift to daughter Judith's husband, William Snead, land now living on, after death, containing 100A on Dunlaps Creek, bond $1,000... Benjamin (X) Haynes...Witness - Patrick Millhollin, Charles Tolbert, Andrew Persinger...Rec'd May 1822.

1:14 - THIS INDENTURE - 24 Feb 1819 - James Merry, Mary wife and Samuel Merry of Botetourt Co. to William Dew of Monroe Co., $1, lot# 58 in Covington, containing 1/4A...James Merry, Samuel Merry, Mary Merry...witness - Moses Persinger, David Hank, James Keans...release of dower by Peter Wright and Joseph D. Keyser justices of peace of Botetourt Co...Rec'd Feb 1822 Oliver Callaghan. Lifted by William Dew 19 Oct 1829.

1:15 - THIS INDENTURE - 10 Jul 1822 - Mathew Wilson, Elizabeth wife, of Bedford Co., to James Burk of Alleghany Co., $1 lot# 16 in town of Covington on Water St. containing 1/4A...Mathew Wilson, Elizabeth Wilson...release of dower by William R. Jones and William R. Porter justices of the peace in Bedford Co....Rec'd Jul 1822 Oliver Callaghan.

1:16 - THIS INDENTURE - 31 Aug 1822 - Alexander Fleet, Elizabeth wife of Alleghany Co. to Nimrod Fachett, $1 for 2 adjoining lots, #'s 67 & 68 in Covington 1/4A each...Alexander Fleet, Elizabeth Fleet...release of dower by Elisha Knox and Charles Callaghan...Rec'd 31 Aug 1822 Oliver Callaghan.

1:17 - THIS INDENTURE - 1 Sept 1823 - Alexander Fleet debtor, to Nash Legrand trustee, both of Alleghany Co. Fleet indebted to James Merry creditor for $64, sold personal property in trust to Nash Legrand. Void if paid by 1 Sept 1824...Alexander Fleet, Nash Legrand...witness - James Burk, David Hank, Ezekiel Rose...Rec'd 3 Sept 1822 Oliver Callaghan.

1:18 - THIS INDENTURE - 16 Sept 1822 - Jacob Persinger to son John Persinger, both of Alleghany Co., $10 for 50A on Potts Creek, granted to Jacob 14 Aug 1799...Jacob Persinger...Rec'd 22 Sept 1822 Oliver Callaghan. Lifted by John A. Carson for heirs of Lee Persinger dec'd 6 Dec 1889. (? & owners)

1:19 - THIS INDENTURE - 8 Oct 1822 - William Herbert administrator of Ferdenando Fairfax of Fairfax Co. VA, to Alexander M. Kerr administrator of George Kerr of the city of Savannah in GA. In consideration and payment of the claim of Alexander M. Kerr admin. against the estate of Ferdenando Fairfax, sold land on Dunlaps Creek in Botetourt Co. and Bath Co., known by Ramsey's Iron Works. Tract was conveyed by Uriah and Sarah Humphries to Edmond Ramsey by deed, 25 Mar 1798, in Botetourt Co., 126A. The tract said to be 25A conveyed by John Robinson to Ramsey and to Adam Fraley, 29 Mar 1797, recorded in Sweet Springs, 2 tracts, part of a larger tract granted originally to Joseph Hunter who conveyed to Uriah Humphries and the other was decreed by, court order to David Robinson, by him to John Robinson, tract with works. The 2 adjoining tracts of 105A & 188A were granted to David Rees, from him to Ramsey by deed, 10 May 1800 and recorded at Sweet Springs. The tract of 71A originally granted to Edmond Ramsey by patent, 15 Mar 17--, the tract of 2A in Monroe Co. Conveyed by Samuel Logue to Ramsey, 22 Feb 1803 recorded Sweet Springs, in Bath Co. 200A conveyed by John Robinson to Ramsey by deed, 28 Oct 1797, 45A tract conveyed by same to same in Botetourt Co., 30 Oct 1797. Also a tract of land granted to Andrew Moore, 29 Oct 1798 conveyed to Ferdenando Fairfax, also 5,000A in Bath Co.,designated by the members in tracts of 1,000A made between William Herbert admin. of Ferdenando Fairfax and Steven Stillwell, ?, Zoper Jarvis, Iven P. Taylor, which deed is recorded to Alexander M. Kerr....William Herbert, admin. of Ferdenando Fairfax...Acknowledged in Fairfax Co. by Richard M. Scott, and George Taylor...Rec'd 2 Oct 1822 Oliver Callaghan.

1:22 - 18 Mar 1822 - Oliver Callaghan appointed clerk of Alleghany Co. - bond - $3,000 by John Callaghan and Charles Callaghan.

15 Apr 1822 - Bond of Nancy Kimberline along with Moses Persinger, Jonathan Kimberline, David Bowyer, Peter Wright, Peter Pence unto the justices, John Holloway, John Callaghan, Michael Arritt, Robert Kincade, and Joseph D. Keyser in the sum of $3,000. The condition is such that Nancy Kimberline is administrator of James Kimberline, to make a true and perfect inventory...Nancy Kimberline, Jonathan Kimberline, Peter Wright, Moses Persinger, David (X) Bowyer. Recorded Oliver Callaghan.

1:23 - 15 Jul 1822 - Bond of George Stull along with John Deeds, Davidson Pitzer in the amount of $300 to the justices, John Callaghan, John Holloway, Robert Kincade, and Michael Arritt, the condition is such that George Stull is administrator of George Stull deceased for a true and perfect inventory of the estate...George Stull, John Deeds, Davidson Pitzer. Rec'd Oliver Callaghan.

1:24 - 9 Aug 1822 - Bond of Henry Figgot along with Joseph D. Keyser, and John Allen in the amount of $500 to justices, Michael Arritt, John Callaghan, Moses H. Mann, Sampson Sawyer, and Elisha ? (probably Knox) as Henry is administrator of ? Smith Sr. deceased to make a true and perfect inventory...Henry Figgot, Joseph D. Keyser, John Allen. Rec'd Aug 1822 Oliver Callaghan.

1:25 - 16 Sept 1822 - Bond of Hamilton Mann along with William Herbert, Samuel Brown, Henry Dressler, and Thomas Byrd in the amount of $4,000 to justices Sampson Sawyer, Charles Callaghan, Jessie Davis, Robert Kincade and John Holloway. As Hamilton Mann is appointed guardian to Archibald Mann and John Mann...Hamilton Mann, Thomas Byrd, Samuel Brown, William Herbert, Henry Dressler. Rec'd Sept 1822 Oliver Callaghan.

16 Sept 1822 - Bond of William Mann, Elisha Knox, and Moses Mann in the amount of $2,000 to justices Sampson Sawyer, Charles Callaghan, Jessie Davis, Robert Kincade and John Holloway. The condition is such that William Mann has been appointed guardian to Sally Mann...William Mann, Elisha Knox, Moses. H. Mann. Teste Oliver Callaghan.

1:26 - Bond of Thomas Richardson and William Richardson in the amount of $250 to justices John Callaghan, Sampson Sawyer, Charles Callaghan, and Moses H. Mann. Thomas has been appointed guardian to Sally Dressler, Peter Dressler, Henry Dressler, and Martha Dressler..Thomas Rhichardson, William Richardson, Adam Dressler. Teste Oliver Callaghan

1:27 - 14 Oct 1822 - Bond of Henry Dressler and Oliver Callaghan in the amount of $300 to the justices, John Callaghan, Sampson Sawyer, Charles Callaghan and Peter Pence. The condition is Henry has been appointed guardian to Charles Dressler, Absolum Dressler, John Dressler, Barbary Dressler, and Malinda Dressler...Henry Tressler, Oliver Callaghan. Rec'd Oct 1822 Oliver Callaghan.

1:28 - THIS INDENTURE - 1 Jan 1821 - Joseph H. Rose and Susan, wife debtor deed of trust to Madison Pitzer. House and lot in Covington to secure sum of money due Richard Smith creditor. Property was advertised for sale 19 Aug 1822. Pitzer appointed Andrew Hamilton to sell property at public auction, was purchase by John Damron...Andrew Hamilton, attorney in fact for Madison Pitzer...Witness - Hamilton Mann, William Herbert, David Kean, and John Crow.

1:29 - THIS INDENTURE - 16 Sept 1822 - William Crawford of Botetourt Co. to Thomas Crawford of Alleghany Co., $200 for 187A lying on Blue Spring Run in Alleghany Co. Rec'd Sept 1822 Oliver Callaghan.

Aug 1822 - Joseph H. Rose, Susan wife debtor, trust deed 1 Jan 1821, recorded Botetourt Co., to Madison Pitzer trustee, lot in Covington to secure debt owed to Richard Smith creditor. Smith having Pitzer sell and act as his attorney...Madison Pitzer...witness - Jacob Fleage. Rec'd Sept 1822 Oliver Callaghan.

1:30 - THIS INDENTURE - 24 Feb 1819 - James Merry, and Mary wife, and Samuel Merry of Botetourt Co. to Joseph Bennett of Monroe Co., 2 lots# 47 & 48, 1/4A each in the Covington...James Merry, Samuel Merry, Mary Merry...witness - James Karnes, Moses Persinger, D. Callaghan...release of dower by Peter Wright and Joseph Keyser.

1:32 - THIS INDENTURE - 10 Jul 1822 - Mathew Wilson, Elizabeth wife of Bedford Co. to Isaac Steel of Alleghany Co., $1 lot# 90 in Covington on Third St. 1/4A...Mathew Wilson, Elizabeth Wilson...release of dower in Bedford Co. by William R. Jones and William R. Porter. Lifted by Isaac Steel 12 Apr 1833.

1:34 - THIS INDENTURE - 10 Jul 1822 - Mathew Wilson, Elizabeth wife of Bedford Co. And James Merry of Alleghany Co., $5 lot# 4 in Covington on Water St. 1/4A...Mathew Wilson, Elizabeth

Wilson...witness - Nash Legrand, Hamilton Mann, Isaac Steel...release of dower in Bedford Co. by William R. Jones and William R. Porter.

1:35 - THIS INDENTURE - 2 Mar 1819 - James Merry, Mary wife and Samuel Merry of Botetourt Co. to J. H. Tachett of Monroe Co., $1 lot# 23 in Covington 1/4A...James Merry, Samuel Merry, Mary Merry...witness ? Hank, Richard Smith, Oliver Callaghan... release of dower in Botetourt Co. by Peter Wright and Joseph D. Keyser.

1:36 - THIS INDENTURE - 13 Nov 1822 - Jacob Persinger and Charles Callaghan, both of Alleghany Co., $60 for 418A, part of a 924A tract on Blue Spring Run...Jacob Persinger...Rec'd Nov 1822 Oliver Callaghan.

1:37 - THIS INDENTURE - 28 Oct 1822 - James Burk debtor, and Nash Legrand trustee both of Alleghany Co. Where as James Burk by obligation, 27 Oct 1822, lands bound to Isaac Steel creditor in penal sum of $534 with a condition for the payment of $267.20, $133.75 part payment 1 May 1823, and $133.75 before 1 Oct 1823. James Burk in consideration of said debt of $267.50 owing to Isaac Steel and for securing the payment to Isaac also in consideration of the sum to James Burk in hand paid by Nash Legrand, land lying Covington lot# 17 1/4...James Burk, Nash Legrand...witness James Merry, T. Wilson, Richard Smith. Rec'd Nov 1822 Oliver Callaghan.

1:39 - THIS INDENTURE - 8 Aug 1822 - John Cook debtor to Elisha Knox Jr. trustee both of Alleghany Co. Cook in order to pay debts to Richard Smith creditor of $174.79, 30 Mar 1819, also bond of $7.32 11 Jan 1821, sells for $1 misc. farm animals and household items...John Cook, Elisha Knox...witness J. Wilson, Elizabeth Mann, Susanna Kelso. Rec'd 16 Nov 1822 Oliver Callaghan.

1:40 - THIS INDENTURE - 10 Jul 1821 - William B. Taylor, collector of Treasury for VA and taxes for US for the 18th district, to Thompson H. Carperton. A tract of land in Monroe Co. was assigned to Nathan Eakins. He was not a resident of the state, tax of 7 cents was not paid. Thompson purchased land for taxes, 8 cents...William B. Taylor...City of Richmond - 18 Jul 1821 Richard A. Carrington and

John H. Exerstance cert'd deed. Rec'd Alleghany Co. 22 Oct 1822 Oliver Callaghan.

1:43 - THIS INDENTURE - 7 Jul 12821 - William B. Taylor, collector of taxes, to Thomas H. Carperton, land in Monroe Co. on Dunlaps Creek 100A, for 16 cents, 20% paid...William B. Taylor...City of Richmond - 10 Jul 1821 Richard A. Carrington and John H. Exerstace cert'd deed. Rec'd in Alleghany Co. 22 Oct 1822 Oliver Callaghan.

1:47 - 19 Nov 1822 - Bond of $3,000 by Nancy Kimberline, John Stone, William Herbert, Patrick Millhollin, John Kimberline, and Dianah Kimberline to the justices, Robert Kincade, Michael Arritt, John Callaghan, Sampson Sawyer, as Nancy is administrator for her deceased husband James Kimberline...Nancy Kimberline, John Stone, William Herbert, Patrick Millhollin, Jonathan Kimberline, and Diannah Kimberline. Rec'd Nov 1822 Oliver Callaghan

THIS INDENTURE - 24 Feb 1819 - James Merry, Mary wife, Samuel Merry of Botetourt Co. to David Hank of Monroe Co., $1 lot# 24 1/4A in Covington...James Merry, Samuel Merry, Mary R. Merry...witness - James Karns, William Dew, Moses Persinger...release of dower 27 Nov 1819 by Peter Wright and Joseph D. Keyser. Rec'd Botetourt Co. 27 Nov 1819, Alleghany Nov 1822 Oliver Callaghan. Lifted by Hank 7 Mar 1842.

1:49 - 15 Oct 1822 - State of OH before Abraham Pukering and John Rickett of Fairfield Co. release of dower by Nancy Butcher...ack'd by Hugh Boyle, clerk of Fairfield Co., John Augustus, associate judge, 16 Oct 1822. (refer to 1:5)

1:50 - THIS INDENTURE - 19 Nov 182? James Merry, Mary wife to John Damron, both of Alleghany Co. $300 lot# 5 1/4A in Covington...James Merry, Mary Merry...release of dower by Peter Pence and John Crow 19 Nov 1822. Rec'd 20 Nov 1822 Oliver Callaghan.

13 Jan 1823 - Bond of $1,000 by John Crow, William Herbert, Samuel Brown, Mathew Sawyer, James Burk. Condition as such is John Crow

appointed coroner...John Crow, William Herbert, Samuel Brown, Mathew Sawyer, James Burk. Rec'd Feb 1823 Oliver Callaghan.

1:52 - 17 Feb 1823 - Bond of $300 by Peter Pence, George Mallow, Thomas Byrd. Condition is as such Thomas Byrd appointed guardian of James Kimberline...Thomas Byrd, George Mallow, Peter Pence. Ack'd Oliver Callaghan.

THIS INDENTURE - 9 Dec 1822 - John Wolf, Magdalene wife to Abraham Wolf, both of Alleghany Co., $50 for 50A located on Potts Creek part of a tract Abraham now lives on...neighbors - Jacob Wolf, William Dew...John (X) Wolf, Magdalene Wolf...witness - William Herbert, Jacob Wolf, Isaac Wolf, William Terry, Jacob Armentrout. Ack'd Mar 1823 Oliver Callaghan.

1:54 - THIS INDENTURE - 10 Oct 1822 - Jacob Bennett, Mary wife to Henry B. Greenwood, both of Alleghany Co., $400 for 50A located on Potts Creek. First granted to Henry Persinger, Mar 1796, sold by Henry to Jacob 13 Dec 1803...neighbors - William Wright, Henry Persinger...Jacob (X) Bennett, Mary (X) Bennett...release of dower by John Callaghan and Stephen Hooks. Rec'd 13 Jan 1823 Oliver Callaghan.

1:56 - THIS INDENTURE - 8 Aug 1822 - Peter Grap, Mary wife, to Adam Dressler, 2/3 their share of Charles Dressler's estate, for $10...Peter (X) Grap Jr., Mary (-) Grap...release of dower by Robert Kincade and Moses H. Mann. Rec'd Sept 1823 Oliver Callaghan.

1:57 - THIS INDENTURE - 12 Apr 1823 - John Rees, Eleanor wife to John Hardy, $1,100 for 122A first conveyed to Rees 21 Nov 1805 located on Dunlaps Creek...John Rees, Eleanor Rees...release of dower by Sampson Sawyer and John Call. Rec'd 12 Apr 1823 Oliver Callaghan.

1:59 - THIS INDENTURE - 12 Apr 1823 - John Hardy, Elizabeth wife debtors, John Callaghan, Sampson Sawyer trustees, and John Rees creditor, all of Alleghany Co. John and Elizabeth indebted to John Rees for $420 to be paid 10 May 1826, by 2 bonds, $270 and $150, $1 paid to John Hardy by John Callaghan and Sampson Sawyer for land on Dunlap's Creek, 120A conveyed to John by deed, Apr 1823 from John Rees, 66A of 125 was granted to Samuel Pogue Sr. by patent 13 Jul 1787...neighbors - William Smith, E. Ramsey...John Hardy, Elizabeth Hardy, John Callaghan, Sampson Sawyer, John Rees. Rec'd 12 Apr 1823 Oliver Callaghan.

1:62 - THIS INDENTURE - 15 Apr 1823 - James Merry, Mary wife, Samuel Merry, to Johnathan Skeene, lot# 54 in Covington for $1, 1/4A...James Merry, Samuel Merry, Mary Merry...Witness - William Harding, Hamilton Mann, and Moses H. Mann. Rec'd Apr 1823 Oliver Callaghan.

THIS INDENTURE - 12 Apr 1823 - Moses H. Mann, trustee of George Sively, a deed of trust executed ? May 1823 by Archibald Morris and ? wife of Alleghany Co., Hazel Williams and Elisha Williams of Bath Co. $2,000 paid by Hazel and Elisha to Moses for 3 tracts now in Alleghany Co. on Jackson River with house that Richard Thomas occupied, 117A, being part of 2 tracts, one of 93A and 270A... Moses H. Mann. Rec'd May 1823 Oliver Callaghan.

1:64 - THIS INDENTURE - 14 ? 1823 - Abraham Pitzer, Mary wife debtor, John Damron admin of Thomas Hardy dec'd creditor, Nash Legrand trustee, all of Alleghany Co. Bond of $80.50 leaves a balance due of a third bond $582.52. Abraham indebted to Thomas Hardy, $1 paid by Nash for land Abraham is living on, 368A on both sides of Cowpasture River. Land conveyed to Pitzer 9 Oct 1810, includes plantation...A. B. Pitzer, Mary Pitzer, John Damron...release of dower by John Holloway and William H. Haynes 15 May 1823. Rec'd 26 May 1823 Oliver Callaghan. Lifted by I. Damron 25 Nov 1830.

1:67 - THIS INDENTURE - 31 May 1823 - William Beverly debtor, Jacob Dressler and James Merry creditor, Henry Conner trustee, all of Alleghany Co. William Beverly indebted to James Merry and Jacob Tressler for $50. Henry Conner paid $1 for misc. farm animals and all household items. Void if paid by 10 Apr 1824...William (X) Beverly, Henry Conner, Jacob Tressler, James Merry...witness - John Hartman, James Brown. Rec'd 31 May 1823 Oliver Callaghan.

1:68 - 19 May 1823 - Bond of Nancy Kimberline, John Callaghan, Dennison Rose, Oliver Callaghan, and Thomas Byrd to Moses H. Mann, Michael Arritt, Stephen Hook, John Persinger, justices for Alleghany Co. in the sum of $1600. Condition as such Nancy is guardian of Elizabeth Ann, Washington, Lorenzo, and Nancy, her children by husband James now dec'd...Nancy Kimberline, Dennison Rose, John Callaghan, Thomas Byrd, Oliver Callaghan. Rec'd 24 Jun 1823 Oliver Callaghan.

1:69 - THIS INDENTURE - 13 Jun 1823- John A. Holly to William Knox, both of Alleghany Co., $1,490 for 160A. Land granted to Moses Mann Sr., then conveyed to Joseph Lewis and from Lewis to Holly...neighbors - William Taylor, Mann and Sively...John A. Holly, Elon (X) Holly. Rec'd 29 Jun 1823 Oliver Callaghan.

1:70 - THIS INDENTURE - 12 Jun 1823 - John A. Holly to William Knox, both of Alleghany Co., $10 paid for 50A (date of 3 Jan 1795)...neighbor - Taylor...John A. Holly, Elon (X) Holly. Rec'd 29 Jun 1823 Oliver Callaghan.

1:71 - THIS INDENTURE - 13 Jun 1823 - William Knox to John A. Holly, both of Alleghany Co., $1,490 for 150A on Oglies Creek, granted to Knox 3 Oct 1789...William Knox. Rec'd 29 Jun 1823 Oliver Callaghan.

1:72 - THIS INDENTURE - 12 Jun 1823 - William Knox to John A. Holly, both of Alleghany Co., $10 for 110A on Oglies Creek, granted to Knox 5 Mar 1812...William Knox. Rec'd 29 Jun 1823 Oliver Callaghan.

1:73 - 16 Jul 1823 - Bond of Charles, Oliver, John and Elisha Knox Jr. are bound unto the President and directors of the Literary Fund in the sum of $2,000. The condition is as such that Charles Callaghan has been elected Treasurer of the board of School Commissioners...Charles Knox, Oliver Knox, John Knox, Elisha Knox. Rec'd Jul 1823 Oliver Callaghan.

THIS INDENTURE - 24 Feb 1819 - James Merry, Mary wife, Samuel Merry of Botetourt Co. to James Walts of Greenbrier Co., $1 lot# 19

1/4A in Covington...James Merry, Samuel Merry, Mary Merry. Rec'd Aug 1823 Oliver Callaghan.

1:74 - John Callaghan against William Knox on a convert. To the Register of Land Office: John Callaghan objects to the register of the land office issue a grant to William Knox for 200A of land on both sides of Oglies Creek joining his own. 1. William did not work in 12 months after survey was made, or return the plat and certificate of land to the land office according to law. 2. Because the breadth of this plat is not 1/3 of its length. 3. Because he has surveyed entirely different from that he entered. That which he entered being on the side of Oglies Creek where as the contrary he surveyed land on Bush Creek and on the section of Howards Creek several miles or more from that land which he entered. 4. Because the said John Callaghan processes a better claim to said land on the water of Bush Creek and on the waters of Howards Creek which said Knox surveyed on the authority of his entry made on Oglies Creek. When he discovered that said John Callaghan had made his entry as follows to wit: John Callaghan enters 200A land part in Greenbrier Co. and part in Bath Co. Including top of Alleghany Mt. where the present road crosses it leading from the Sulphur Springs to Covington and where the new turnpike road is to cross said mountain to begin 30 poles west the forks of the road leading to the Sweet Springs and extending east on both sides of the road for quantity and enter the same on a land office Treasury warrant for 200A #7087, 28 May 1821. Date of above entry 25 Jun 1821. 5. When William discovered Callaghan had entered said land he rumored and reported that he had entered it before Callaghan. In order to confirm those rumors and reports Knox in place of surveying the land which he did enter on Oglies Creek he surveyed the land that said Callaghan had entered on waters of Bush Creek and Howards Creek, 7 miles more distant from the land he entered which proceeding deceived and copied land Callaghan and prevented him from surveying on the authority and virtue of the above mentioned warrant. 6. Because where the said Callgahan found that he had been deceived by Knox he renters said land of Bush and Howards Creek, to wit: 200A land by a transfer from the Surveyors Office of Greenbrier Co. The land partly in Greenbrier and partly in Bath, that part now in Alleghany Co. Including the top of Alleghany Mt. where the present road crosses leading from this. Land Office Treasury Warrant 200A #7087 28 May

1823, date on William Knox's entry 24 Jun 1823...18 Nov 1823 Jessie Davis.

1:76 - THIS INDENTURE - 22 Jan 1822 - between John Robinson of Gallia Co. OH to George Claypool of Jackson Co. VA., $100 for 150A in Bath Co. Granted to John 11 Aug 1796 on Dunlaps Creek on the south end of Lick Mt...John Robinson. Recorded in Gallia 23 Jan 1822 by Ed McMillen and Francis Leclervy. Recorded 26 Feb 1824 Oliver Callaghan.

1:78 - THIS INDENTURE - 1 Jan 1823 - between Charles Callaghan, Nancy wife to Ephraim Simmons both of Alleghany Co., $100 for 363A on Potts Creek...neighbors - William Humphries, and Jacob Wolf...Charles Callaghan, Agnes Callaghan. Recorded 30 Apr 1823 Oliver Callaghan. Lifted by E. Simmons 16 Jun 1834.

1:79 - 19 Aug 1823 - John Holloway, Oliver, John, and Charles Callaghan, William H. Haynes, David Kean, Samuel Brown, and Alexander Blair are bound unto James Pleasant Jr. Esquire Governor of VA in the sum of $30,000. Condition is as such that John Holloway appointed Sheriff of Alleghany Co. 1 Jul 1823.

1:81 - 15 Sept 1823 - John Persinger, Peter Pence, Thomas Byrd, and Anthony Brunnemer are bound unto the Governor of VA in the amount of $1,000. Condition as such that John Persinger is appointed Commissioner of Revenue for Alleghany Co.

1:82 - THIS INDENTURE - 20 Aug 1823 - Jacob Mallow, Catherine wife to John Mallow both of Alleghany Co., $48 for 6A in Jackson River joining Michael Mallow and Dressler...Jacob Mallow, Catherine Mallow. Rec'd 4 Sept 1823 Oliver Callaghan.

1:83 - THIS INDENTURE - 20 Aug 1823 - Jacob Mallow, Cathy wife of Alleghany Co. to John Sparks of Madison Co. VA., $1,000 for 99A on the south side of Jackson River joining Michael Mallow. Part of 232A tract which Jacob now lives on...Jacob Mallow, Catherine Mallow. Rec'd 4 Sept 1823 Oliver Callaghan.

1:84 - 3 Oct 1823 - Beniah Hutchinson, Lewis Stuart, and Archibald Hutchinson are bound to the Governor of VA in the sum of $10,000. Condition as such, Beniah Hutchinson appointed clerk of Superior court of law of Alleghany by James Allen, judge of Superior Court. Rec'd 6 Oct 1823 Oliver Callaghan.

1:86 - 24 Sept 1823 - Peter Circle dec'd, of Botetourt devised land in Botetourt on Cowpasture River and Simpsons Creek to son Andrew, son-in-law Jacob Nicely and wife Magdalena (Circle). Land was orginally surveyed for John Robinson and John Lewis on 3 Apr 1746 containing 300A, it became vested in John Handley who conveyed to Peter Circle 6 Feb 1799. Andrew and Elizabeth Circle, Jacob and Magdalena Nicely now of Alleghany Co. sell to Stephen Hook of Bath Co. for $1,350, 142 A...Andrew Circle, Elizabeth Circle, Jacob Nicely, Magdelena Nicely...witness - James Cox, George Lemon, and Joseph D. Keyser...ack'd by Joseph D. Keyser and Boston Harnsbarger 24 Sept 1823...release of dower by Oliver Callaghan. Lifted by Eli Hook 26 Sept 1829.

THIS INDENTURE - 19 Jul 1823 - Orlando Griffith, Lucy wife of Bath Co. to Samuel Crawford of Botetourt Co., $750.50 for 117A located on Cowpasture River part of 190A conveyed to Griffith by Robert and Andrew Crawford 14 Oct 1818...Orlando Griffith, Lucy Griffith...Ack'd by William H. Haynes and John Holloway, 19 Jul 1823...release of dower by Oliver Callaghan.

1:89 - THIS INDENTURE - 19 Jul 1823- Orlando Griffith, Lucy wife of Bath Co. to Conrad Lemon of Alleghany Co., $250 for 69A part of 190A tract conveyed same as above...Orlando Griffith, Lucy Griffith...release of dower by William H. Haynes and John Holloway 19 Jul 1823. Rec'd Nov 1823 Oliver Callaghan.

1:91 - THIS INDENTURE - 31 Aug 1822 - Alex McClintic, Sarah wife , Alice Cavendish, all of Bath Co., William T. Mann, Margaret wife of Greenbirer Co., to George Sively of Alleghany Co. $1 for 3/6 part of 400A in Alleghany Co. on Cold Spring Run, granted to Archibald Mann dec'd, and decending to Moses, John, William T. Mann, Alice Cavendish, Jame W. McClintic, and Sarah W. McClintic, represt of Archibald Mann...Alex McClintic, Sarah McClintic, Alice Cavendish,

William T. Mann, Margaret Mann...release of dower in Bath Co. by William McDean, and William McClintic 21 Sept 1822...release of dower in Greenbrier Co. by James Withrow, and James McLaughlin, 16 Jan 1823. Rec'd 1 Jan 1824 Oliver Calleghan.

1:93 - THIS INDENTURE - 21 Oct 1816 - Samuel Porter, Sarah wife to John Deeds both of Botetourt Co., $600 for 55A in Rich Patch, and 10A part of a second tract...neighbors - Michael Kimberline and Crawford...witness - William Womack, John Holloway, and John Pitzer...Samuel Porter, Sarah Porter..release of dower by John Holloway and John Pitzer 28 Oct 1816. Rec'd 15 Dec 1823 Oliver Callaghan.

1:94 - THIS INDENTURE - 1 Oct 1817 - George Lemon to Thomas Hardy both of Botetourt Co., $50 for 32A to make good deed of conveyance before 1 Oct 1848. Thomas Hardy departed life intestate before convance leaving heirs Thomas, John, Jacob, Samuel and the heirs of George Hardy dec'd, five daughters - Polly who married John Damron, Rebecca, who married Meshach Smith, Sarah who married Daniel Sizer, Beckey who married Abner Sisson, and Ann who married Armistead Sisson. George Hardy departing this life intestate before his father and having four children, Barkely, William, George, and Sarah...Jan 1824 - between George and Nancy Lemon of Alleghany Co. and the above named heirs of Thomas Hardy dec'd. $5 for 32A on Cowpasture River part of a grant of 134A to George Lemon by patent (no date)...neighbors - Hardy...George Lemon, Nancy Lemon...witness - Joseph D. Keyser, Sebastian Hansbarger...release of dower by Joseph D. Keyser and Sebastian Hansbarger. Rec'd in Feb 1824 Oliver Callaghan.

1:96 - 16 Feb 1824 - William Herbert and James Merry bond to Peter Pence, Charles Callaghan, John Callaghan, and John Persinger justices. The condition of obligation is that William Herbert has been appointed guardian to Polly Withers...William Herbert, James Merry...teste Oliver Callaghan.

1:97 THIS INDENTURE - 3 May 1823 - Joseph Pinnell, Harriet wife to Dennison Rose both of Alleghany Co., $50 for 50A on Persingers Run. Orginal patent granted to Christopher Shaver 6 Oct 1804,

Christopher and Mary wife conveyed to Jacob Persinger, Jacob and Margaret wife conveyed to Lewis Circle and by Lewis and Martha L. wife to Joseph Pinnell, 20 Feb 1819...Joseph Pinnell, Harriet Pinnell...witness - Alexander Rayhill, Achilles Dew, John Howard...release of dower by Michael Arritt and John Arritt. Rec'd Feb 1824 Oliver Callaghan.

1:98 - THIS INDENTURE - 3 May 1823 - Joseph Pinnell and Harriet wife to Denison Rose all of Alleghany Co., $100 for 227A on Potts Creek, patent for Henry Persinger, 10 May 1798. Henry and wife, Griselda sold to Christopher Shaver and wife, they in turn sold to Jacob Persinger, who sold to Jacob and Margaret Persinger, who in turn sold to Lewis Circle, Lewis and Martha L. sold to Joseph Pinnell, 27 Feb 1819...neighbor Henry Persinger...witness - Archilles Dew, Alexander Rayhill, John Howard...Joseph Pinnell, Harriet Pinnell...release of dower by Michael and John Arritt, 4 Jul 1823. Rec'd Feb 1824 Oliver Callaghan. Lifted by Denison Rose 22 Jul 1837.

1:100 - 24 Sept 1823 - Peter Circle dec'd of Botetourt Co., by his will left land on Cowpasture and Potts Creek to his son, Andrew Circle and to son-in-law Louis Jacob Nicely and wife Magdalane. Land orginally surveyed for John Robinson and John Lewis, 3 Apr 1746, 300A, the property became vested in John Handley who conveyed to Circle, dec'd, 16 Feb 1799, also Andrew and Jacob Niceley have agreed to divide the land.
THIS INDENTURE - between Andrew Circle, Elizabeth wife to Jacob Nicely, Magdalena wife, $5 for 142A on Simpsons Creek...Andrew Circle, Elizabeth Circle...witness - Eli Hook, George Lemon, James Cox...note the said tarct of 300A when accurately surveyed only contains 284A...release of dower by Boston Hansbarger and Joseph D. Keyser, 24 Sept 1823. Lifted by J. Nicely 18 Mar 1828.

1:102 - THIS INDENTURE - 14 Mar 1823 - James Kincade, Phebe wife of Greenbrier Co. to Andrew Kincade of Alleghany Co., $1 for 2 tracts, first 20A on Jackson River, second 30A...James Kincade, Phebe Kincade...neighbor Alice Cavender... release of dower by Robert Kincade and Moses H. Mann, 14 Mar 1823. Rec'd 19 Jan 1824 Oliver Callaghan. Lifted by Andrew Kincade 31 Dec 1828.

1:104 - THIS INDENTURE - 14 Mar 1823 - James Kincade, Phebe wife of Greenbrier Co. to Andrew Kincade of Alleghany Co., $1 for their interest in shares of James and Ann Kincade. William Kincade conveyed to James Kincade by deed recorded in Bath Co., 2 tracts, one containing 110A and the other 98A in Alleghany Co. on Jackson River...James Kincade, Phebe Kincade...release of dower by Robert Kincade and Moses H. Mann, 14 Mar 1823. Rec'd 19 Jan 1824 Oliver Callaghan.

1:105 - THIS INDENTURE - 2 Jun 1823 - Nimrod Tackitt, Ann wife of Monroe Co. to Alexander Fleet of Alleghany Co., $1 for 2 lots# 67 & 68 1/4A each in Covington...Nimrod Tackitt, Ann Tackitt...ack'd in Greenbrier Co. 5 Jul 1823, Henry Alexander and James Hanley...release of dower by Oliver Callaghan. Rec'd Mar 1824 Oliver Callaghan.

1:106 - 3 Jul 1823 - Land division of Charles Dressler dec'd with widows thirds - widow 106A, lots by drawing - Charlotte Dressler 17A, Barbara Dressler 13A, Charles Dressler 12A, Absolom Dressler 12A, Adam Dressler 12A, Sarah Dressler 12A, Thomas Richardson 16A, Adam Dressler 25A, Martha Dressler 51A, Adam Dressler 24A, Peter Dressler 31A, Milinda Dressler 11A, John Dressler 12A, Henry Dressler 13A. (refer 1: 26 & 56)
Rec'd Jun 1824 Oliver Callaghan. Lifted by Peter Dressler 19 Jan 1835.

1:109 - 22 Jun 1824 - Bond of $1,500 given for John A.Vanlear by Joseph D. Keyser, William H. Terrill. Condition of bond is such that John obtained license to celebrate the rites of matrimony agreeable to the form and ceremonies of the Presbyterian Church...John A. Vanlear, Joseph D. Keyser, William H. Terrill. Rec'd Jun 1824 Oliver Callaghan.

1:110 - 12 Apr 1824 - Land laid off for Katherine, widow of George Meyers on Dunlap Creek, 40A...neighbor - Elisha Knox Sr...Charles Callaghan, Elisha Knox, John Callaghan. Rec'd May 1824 Oliver Callaghan.

THIS INDENTURE - 19 Apr 1824 - James Merry, Mary R. wife of Alleghany Co. to Andrew Scott or Rockbridge Co., $1 for lot# 53 1/4A in Covington...James Merry, Mary R. Merry. Rec'd 20 Apr 1824 Oliver Callaghan.

1:111 - THIS INDENTURE - 27 Mar 1824 - Orlando Griffith, Lucy wife of Bath Co. to George Armontrout of Alleghany Co., $74.22 for 15A Cowpasture River...neighbor - Crawford...Orlando Griffith, Lucy Griffith...release of dower by James D. Keyser and Peter Pence. Rec'd May 1824 Oliver Callaghan.

1:112 - THIS INDENTURE - 20 Apr 1824 - James Merry, Mary wife and Samuel Merry of Alleghany Co. to Elisha B. Williams of Bath Co., lots # 29 & 30 1/4A each in Covington...James Merry, Mary Merry, Samuel Merry...witness - Richard Smith, D. Callaghan, Benjamin T. Douglas. Rec'd May 1824 Oliver Callaghan.

1:113 - THIS INDENTURE - 31 Jan 1824 - Druna Foster, Sarah wife to Isaac Gray, $50 for 1/5 part of a tract belonging to George Hardy dec'd on Roaring Run and Rich Patch, part of 190A granted to Stephen Moore assignee of Jereamiah B. Bell who was assignee of John Newell now dec'd by patent 23 Jun 1797, then by heirs of Stephen Moore conveyed to George Hardy...Druna Foster, Sally (X) Foster...release of dower by Stephen Hook and Peter Pence 31 Jan 1824. Rec'd Apr 1824 Oliver Callaghan.

1:114 - THIS INDENTURE - 28 Jan 1824 - Mathew D. Brown of Mason Co. VA to Patrick Millhollin of Alleghany Co., $119 now with $200 to be paid on 25 Dec 1825 for 80A, Island Ford Plantation on Jackson River...Mathew Brown...witness - J. H. Holloway, and William G. Holloway. Rec'd Jun 1824 Oliver Callaghan. Lifted by D. P. ? (looks like Cump) 16 Jun 1845.

1:116 - THIS INDENTURE - 11 May 1824 - Jacob Wanstruf, Catherine wife of Pendleton Co. to John Rinehard of Botetourt Co., $1 for first tract of 107A on Potts Creek in Alleghany Co., part of a survey of 395A first granted to John Brown and William Brown, by James Breckenridge as attorney for John Brown conveyed to Phillip Fisher by deed 15 Jan 1808...neighbors - Henry Smith and Ester Rayhill. Second tract 50A granted to Phillip Fisher as assignee of Henry Smith by patent bearing date 2 Apr 1808. The 50A tract has been interlaid as part of a 300A tract belonging to Michael ?. The third tract of 12A granted to Phillip Fisher by patent 28 Oct 1807...neighbors - Brown and Smith...Jacob Wanstruf, Catherine (X) Wanstruf...witness - in Pendleton Co. Henry Hull and William Dyer, 11 May 1824...release of dower by Henry Hull and William Dyer. Rec'd 17 May 1824 Oliver Callaghan. Lifted by M. Arritt 21 Jan 1828.

1:118 - 19 Mar 1818 - Articles of agreement between David Maggard Sr. and Adam Maggard both of Monroe Co. David Sr. leased plantation, mills, garden and flax patch to David. Adam is to have all the penny fit of the plantation, and use of 3 horses, when David or his wife need a horse they have the privilege. Adam is to feed 5 head of cattle. David Sr. reserves all the building about the house where he now lives and 1 stable and ½ orchard. Adam is to have all above mentioned articles during said David Sr.'s life and at his decease Adam is to have plantation, mill and all for which Adam is to pay $1,000 to other legatees. He has 7 yrs to pay. We each bind ourseleves inthe sum of $2,000...David Maggard, Adam Maggard...witness - Jacob Persinger Sr., Joseph Maggard. Rec'd 17 May 1824 Oliver Callaghan.

1:119 - 12 Nov 1823 - Nicholas Vanstavern of Monroe Co. to Cornelius Vanstavern of Alleghany Co., misc. household furniture, 12 law books. All this for the purpose to make him my security to William Vanstavern for $105 which I borrowed in the 1820 and to secure to Cornelius $50 I have owed him since May 1821, also ad my security to Michael Erskine for $50... Nicholas Vanstavern...witness - W. Haws, William Snead. Rec'd Jun 1824 Oliver Callaghan.

15 Mar 1824 - To brother Cornelius Vanstavern, please receive from my father Nicholas Vanstavern the following property (which he has this day sold to me), 1 shot gun, 12 siliver spoons, 2 beds, and misc furniture, books, "Munfords General Index, Gilberts Law of Evidence (2 vols), Washingtons Reports, and 2 vols of Calls Reports, The Pleaders Assistant, Gilberts Republican," please oblige your brother...William Vanstavern. Rec'd Cornelius Vanstavern. Rec'd Jun 1824 Oliver Callaghan.

1:120 - 19 Nov 1823 - I do give unto the heirs of Henry Wetson of Bath Co., 1 cow called "beeflow" and her increase forever, naming them as follows, Franklin, Dorsey, Pulina, Vauen?, and Elizabeth...Michael Mallow (in dutch)...witness - Richard Smith, James Gants. Rec'd Jun 1824 Oliver Callaghan.

THIS INDENTURE - 24 Feb 1819 - James Merry and Mary wife, Samuel Merry of Botetourt Co, to William Mann of Bath Co., $1 for lot# 43 & 44 in Covington 1/4A each...James Merry, Samuel Merry, Mary Merry...witness - Richard Smith, D. Callaghan, Ben R. Douglas...release of dower by Peter Wright and Joseph D. Keyser. Rec'd Jun 1824 Oliver Callaghan.

1:121 - THIS INDENTURE - 11 Aug 1823 - between Charles Tolbert debtor and Charles Callaghan trustee, both of Alleghany Co., in order to secure and indemnify James Merry creditor, and to secure certain debts due to Richard Smith creditor, and the said James Merry in consideration of $1 paid to Tolbert by Callaghan misc. farm animals and household items were placed in trust...Charles Tolbert...Charles Callaghan. Rec'd July 1824 Oliver Callaghan.

1:122 - 19 Jul 1824 - Charles Callaghan, James Merry, Isaac Johnson, bond to Peter Pence, William H. Haynes, Stephen Hooks, and Sampson Sawyer, justices of Alleghany Co. Condition as such Charles Callaghan appointed gurardian to Julia Callaghan infant heir of Dennis Callaghan dec'd...Charles Callaghan, Isaac Johnson, James Merry...witness - Oliver Callaghan.

THIS INDENTURE - 19 Jul 1824 - Jacob Hansbarger to Sebastian Hansbarger both of Alleghany Co., $400 for land on Wilson's Creek, being whole share of Jacob's land by deed of gift from John Hansbarger his father, 23 Aug 1809, recorded in Bath Co. Land between John (father) and Sebastian held and owned by them by same deed of gift...Jacob Hansbarger...witness - John Holloway, Lewis T. Mann. Rec'd Jul 1824 Oliver Callaghan.

1:123 - THIS INDENTURE - 2 May 1817 - Archibald Reed, Susanna, wife of Botetourt Co. to Samuel Irwin of Alleghany Co., $50 for 188A part of a tract of 750A granted to Thomas Davis and George Drumond.

21

Drumond conveyed tract of 188A to Archibald Reed, Archibald conveyed to Irwin, 11 Apr 1814. Land in Rich Patch on Blue Spr Run...Archibald Reed, Susanna Reed...release of dower by John Holloway and John Pitzer in Botetourt Co. Rec'd Aug term 1824 Oliver Callaghan. Patent dates for this indenture are blank.

1:125 - THIS INDENTURE - 17 May 1824 - William Johnson, Susanna wife to Jacob Wolf both of Allaghany Co., $400 for land in Rich Patch on Potts Creek, part of tract of land bought by Robert Harvey and conveyed to Gillaspie, 1798, and conveyed to Porter by Gillaspie, 10 Jul 1801...neighbors - Robert Voyers, and Persinger...William Johnson, Susanna Johnson...release of dower by Michael Arritt and John Arritt. Rec'd Aug term Oliver Callaghan.

1:126 - THIS INDENTURE - 17 Aug 1824 - Beniah Hutchinson, who was appointed by decree of Chancery Court a Commission for the purpose, on behalf of John Knox, William Knox, and Nelson Knox, infants and heirs of John Knox dec'd and under 21 yrs. Pursuance of decree of Chancery, 20 Oct 1823, depending between Elisha Knox plaintiff and infants of John Knox and Hannah Knox defendants. It was adjudged that infants, by Beniah, convey unto Elisha by deed with special warranty certain lands, 150A survey, 1 Apr 1809, in Alleghany Co., on Dunlaps Creek patented to John Knox, 6 aug 1810...neighbors - Elisha Knox, Bernard Pitzer...Beniah Hutchinson. Rec'd Aug 1824 Oliver Callaghan.

1:128 - THIS INDENTURE - 17 Jun 1824 - William Richardson, Elizabeth wife, Thomas R. Richardson, Margaret wife, of Alleghany Co. to John Peyton of Augusta Co., $300 for 276A in Falling Spring Valley. Land first granted to William and Thomas Richardson by patent 13 Nov 1818...neighbors - Henry Massie and Moses Mann...William Richardson, Elizabeth (O) Richardson, Thomas Richardson, Margaret Richardson...release of dowers by Robert Kincaid and Jessie Davis, 17 Jun 1824. Rec'd Sept 1824 Oliver Callaghan.

1:129 - THIS INDENTURE - 10 Jul 1824 - William Daval of Buckingham Co. to William H. B. Christian of Campbell Co. William Daval through love and affection for William H. B. Christian sells for $1, 653A part of 900A land patented 13 Sept 1793 to Christopher

McPherson, on Henley's Mill Creek in Botetourt Co., now Alleghany Co. McPherson conveyed to William Duval rec'd in General Court VA ...neighbors - Armentrout, George and Peter Circle...William Duval...Witness - Henry Flood, Phillip Duval, Owens C. Fowler...Ack'd in Buckingham Co., 10 Jul 1824 by Henry Flood and William Duval. Rec'd Sept 1824 Oliver Callaghan.

1:131 - THIS INDENTURE - 12 Jul 1824 - William H. B. Christian, Saluda B. wife of Campbell Co. to William Morgan of the town of Lynchburg. Morgan paid $267.73 for 650A on Henley Mill Creek on Cow Pasture River...neighbor - George Armentrout...William H. B. Christian, Salada B. Christian...release of dower in Campbell Co. by Thomas Discon and John McAllister, 20 Jul 1824. Rec'd Sept 1824 Oliver Callaghan.

1:132 - THIS INDENTURE - 27 Jan 1824 - between Samuel Merry of St. Louis Missouri and James Merry of Alleghany Co., $1 for land he and Samuel purchased from George Penlying on Jackson River on which Covington is laid off containing 138A...neighbors - Peter Wright...Samuel Merry...witness - J. Hartman, George H. Payne, I. Wilson. Rec'd Sept 1824 Oliver Callaghan. Lifted by Maj. Robert Kelso 16 Oct 1828.

1:133 - THIS INDENTURE - 13 Sept 1824 - James Merry, Mary wife to Samuel B. Lowrey both of Alleghany Co., $1 for lot # 76 in Covington 1/4A...James Merry, Mary R. Merry. Rec'd Sept 1824 Oliver Callaghan.

1:134 - THIS INDENTURE - _ _ 1824 - William Mann to Moses H. Mann. Moses paid $600 for 132A part of a tract of 835A first granted to Moses Mann dec'd father of said William Mann on the east side of Jackson River...William Mann. Rec'd Sept 1824 Oliver Callaghan.

1:135 - Bond of $1,000 given by Patrick Millhollin, George Mallow, and Peter Pence. The condition is such that Patrick Millhollin is appointed Commissioner of Public Revenue for the year of 1825...Patrick Millhollin, George Mallow, Peter Pence. Rec'd 20 Sept 1824 Oliver Callaghan.

THIS INDENTURE - 12 Aug 1824 - Jacob Carrigan, Mary wife of Martick township in Lancaster PA to Jacob Harnsbarger of Alleghany Co., farmer. Jacob paid $1,250 for 2 tracts, 24A and 30A. First owned by Patrick Carrigan dec'd and wife Mary by his will 21 Mar 1793, his beloved relation, Jacob Carrigan son of Michael Carrigan of PA. Mary also deceased...Jacob (X) Carrigan, Mary (X) Carrigan...witness - Nathan Lightner, John Reigart...release of dower in Lancaster by Nathan Lightner, 25 Aug 1824. Rec'd Oct 1824 Oliver Callaghan.

1:138 - THIS INDENTURE - 18 Oct 1824 - James Merry, Mary wife to Isaac Steele both of Alleghany Co., $1 for 2 lots # 113 & 114 in Covington, 1/4A each...James Merry, Mary Merry. Rec'd 1824 Oliver Callaghan. Lifted by I. Steele 12 Apr 1833.

THIS INDENTURE - 18 Oct 1814 - James Merry, Mary wife to James Keans, both of Alleghany Co., lot # 80 in Covington, 1/4A...James Merry, Mary Merry. Rec'd Nov 1824 Oliver Callaghan.

1:139 - THIS INDENTURE - 25 Sept 1824 - George Sawyer to James Merry, William H. Terrill, Andrew Travers (who is executor of Sampson Sawyer dec'd). George Sawyer in debt to Andrew Travers, as executor, in the sum of $450.80 payable before 25 Mar 1826. Also in the further sum of $100 which George paid on 25 Dec 1824. James and William paid $1 for land on Dunlaps Creek, 71A, which George claimed by purchase from his father, which was decreed to be sold by the Chancellor in Lewisburg, 10 Jun 1824, for the benifit of Andrew Swayer Jr. He was exonerated from the operation of the decree upon certain conditions which may be seen by reference to an article of agreement entered into between George and Andrew and placed in the hands of James Merry for safe keeping...George Sawyer, James Merry, William H. Terrill...witness - William Scott, James Sawyer, Mathew Sawyer. Rec'd 19 Oct 1824 Oliver Callaghan.

1:141 - THIS INDENTURE - William Beverly debtor to Elisha Knox trustee, both of Alleghany Co. William in order to secure payments of a debt of $51.75 with interest thereon to James Merry creditor, $1 paid for misc. farm animals, and household furniture...William (X) Beverly, Elisha Knox Jr. Rec'd 16 Nov 1824 Oliver Callaghan.

1:142 - THIS INDENTURE - 16 Nov 1824 - James Merry, Mary wife to Henry Dressler, both of Allehgany Co., $1 for lot # 120 in Covington, 1/4A...James Merry, Mary R. Merry. Rec'd Nov 1824 Oliver Callaghan.

15 Nov 1824 - John H. Peyton and William McClintic, bond to Moses H. Mann, Sampson Sawyer, Isaac Steel, and Charles Callaghan justices of Alleghany Co. in the sum of $4,800. Condition of the bond is that John H. Peyton has been appointed guardian to Benjamin Lewis...John H. Peyton, William McClintic...Teste - Oliver Callaghan.

1:143 - Bond by Harvey Sawyer, Oliver Callaghan, David Hank, Jacob Fudge, and James Burk in the sum of $1,500. Condition is that Harvey Sawyer obtained a license to celebrate the rites of matrimony for the Methodist Episcopal Church...Harvey Sawyer, Oliver Callaghan, James Burk, David Hank, Jacob Fudge...Teste Oliver Callaghan.

THIS INDENTURE - 13 Dec 1824 - Jacob Persinger of Green Co. OH to the heirs of Moses Persinger dec'd of Alleghany Co., ½ of a tract granted to Jacob and Moses, 15 Mar 1808, 75A on Potts Creek...Jacob Persinger. Rec'd 17 Dec 1824 Oliver Callaghan * heirs of Lee Persinger dec'd are the present owners of the land described in this deed, date written unknown.

1:144 - 9 Sept 1823 - At court held in Bath Co. on the motion of George Knight a mulatto man free born, it is ordered that the clerk furnish George with a copy of the above facts...Charles L. Francisco, clerk. Rec'd 20 Dec 1824 Oliver Callaghan.

THIS INDENTURE - 8 Jan 1823 - Henry Dressler, Elizabeth wife to John Taylor both of Alleghany Co., $50 for lot # 120 in Covington, 1/4A...Henry Dressler, Elizabeth Dressler...release of dower by John Callaghan and Jessie Davis 8 Jan 1825. Rec'd Jan 1825 Oliver Callaghan.

1:145 - 11 Jan 1825 - Thomas T. White debtor, Patrick Millhollin trustee, and Silas G. Latham creditor, all of Alleghany Co. White indebted to Latham for $94.56 money lent. To pay debt he placed in trust to Patrick interest in crop of tabacco, misc. farm animals, and household furniture...Thomas T. White, Patrick Millhollin, Silas G. Latham...Teste - William H. Davis, Obadiah (X) Reynolds, William Matherny. Rec'd Feb 1825 Oliver Callaghan.

1:146 - 6 Jan ? - William Matheny debtor, Thomas T. White trustee, and Rebecca Matheny creditor, all of Alleghany Co. William indebeted to Rebecca for $300 for 16 years of services rendered by said Rebecca. William places in trust to White misc farm animals and equipment, also present growing crop of wheat...William Matheny, Thomas White, Rebecca (X) Matheny...Teste Silas G. Latham. Rec'd Feb 1825 Oliver Callaghan. Lifted by T. White 21 Jan 1826.

1:147 - THIS INDENTURE - 13 Dec 1824 - Sebastian Hansbarger, Elizabeth wife, and John Hansbarger, both of Alleghany Co., $1 for 11 A on Wilsons Creek, upper tract of land conveyed by gift from John Hansbarger Sr. to Jacob Hansbarger. Deed in Bath Co. 23 Aug 1809 and conveyed by Jacob to Sebastian, deed in Alleghany Co. 1824...Sebastian Hansbarger, Elizabeth Hansbarger...witness - Joseph D. Keyser, William H. Haynes...release of dower by Joseph D. Keyser and William H. Haynes. Rec'd Feb 1825 Oliver Callaghan.

1:149 - THIS INDENTURE - 10 Jul 1822 - Mathew Wilson, Elizabeth wife of Bedford Co. to Peter Pence of Alleghany Co., $1 for lot # 89 on Bath St. in Covington 1/4A...Mathew Wilson, Elizabeth Wilson...witness - Jacob Tressler, Andrew Hamilton, Henry Tressler...release of dower by William R. Jones and William R. Porter in Bedford Co. Rec'd 17 Jan 1825 Oliver Callaghan.

1:150 - 21 Feb 1828 - Bond of John and Michael Mallow to Joseph Damron, Sampson Sawyers, William H. Haynes, and Charles Callaghan, in the amount of $500. The condition is such that John Mallow is appointed guardian of Joanah and Manza Jane Brunnemer...John Mallow, Michael (X) Mallow...Teste Oliver Callaghan.

THIS INDENTURE - 21 Feb 1824 - George Mallow, Catherine wife to Michael Mallow Sr. both of Alleghany Co. Lot # 8,20,12, part of Henry Dresslers, dec'd, old tract of land in Alleghany between land of Conrad Fudge and John Brunnemer on Jackson River. Lot #8 part of 170A containing 3 3/4A, lot # 20 part of same tract of 170A containing 1A,

20 poles. Lot # 12 part of a tract held by Henry Dressler dec'd containing 200A, contains 9 3/4A. The first lot joining Moses Dressler. The said 3 lots of land being the dividend of George Mallow and Catherine, out of the 2 above named tracts...George Mallow, no signature for Catherine. Rec'd 21 Feb 1825 Oliver Callaghan.

1:152 - THE REGISTER of the land office of the State of Virginia - James Knox objects to the register of the land office issue a grant to David Lockhart for 40A on Oglies Creek adjoining his own land and land of heirs of Dennis Callaghan dec'd to begin at the Rock Lick and to extend up his southeast line for quantity by part of an exhange land office Treasurary Warrant for 1,000A #1754 assigned to John Long dated 18 Jun 1823. Knox objects that the warrant above mentioned by virtue of which said Lockhart made his ? and location was orginally issued to John Long and assigned from said Long to James Brown who was the proper owner of warrant but that the said Lockhart had gotten any assignment of the warrant from the said Samuel Brown for 40A and failed to get an assignment for the 40A until _ Dec in year aforesaid. James Knox claims a better right to the land by virtue of an entry and location in these words: James Knoxs enters 50A land on Oglies Creek adjoining land of David Lockhart. Beginning at the upper end of John Callaghan and running along David Lockharts southeast line for quantity by part of a land office Tresuary Warrant for 200A #7466 dated 1 Dec 1823 previous to date of assignment from Samuel Brown to David Lockhart...Filed land office 5 Jun 1824...Teste William Selden.

1:153 -THE REGISTER of the Land Office in the State of Virginia - Charles Callaghan objects to the Register of the Land Office issuing a grant to Samuel Brown and Abraham Bishop for 138A of land in Alleghany Co. on the north fork of Oglies Creek, the survey of which bears date on the 29 July 1824 for the following reasons, to wit: that Samuel Brown moiety (share) of the said 138A was made by virtue of, and on a Land Office exchange Treasury Warrant for 300A #1758 assigned of John Long, the warrant aforesaid issued to John Long in the year 1805 and was in the same year assigned from John Long to James Brown, that James Brown since the date of the assignment aforesaid departed this life, leaving the warrant aforesaid unappropriated and in the surveyors office of Bath Co., that the said

Samuel Brown got the warrant aforesaid from the surveyor of Bath Co. and receipted to the surveyor of Bath Co. for it as the surviving heir of James Brown dec'd and then altered the name (James) in said assignment to Samuel as is seen by his receipt to the Surveyor of Bath Co. by virtue of which alteration he the said Samuel Brown claims the warrant aforesaid and on which he made the following locations: "Samuel Brown and Abraham Bishop enters 600A of land in Alleghany Co. on the north fork of Oglies Creek. Beginning at the land of J. Johnson, then extending up said branch and over on the ridge between said fork and the south fork of Oglies Creek for quantity, Brown's moiety by a land office exchange Treasuary Warrant for 300A #1758 assignee of John Long, part of Bishops moiety by a land office Treasuary Warrant for 100A #7393 assignee of John Crow. The residue, 200A, by part of a land office Exchange Warrant for 1,000A assignee of Henry Anderson and James Ragland." Bishops warrant being good there is no objection as to his part, on which said entry a survey has been made of 138A bearing date as above and the entry dated 3 Aug 1822. The said Charles Callaghan enters 100A of the land aforesaid as follows: 22 Sept 1824, Charles Callghan enters 100A of land in Alleghany Co. On the north fork of Uglies Creek a branch of Dunlaps Creek, beginning at the upper end of the land of Isaac Johnson from thence extending up the creek for quantity by three land office treasuary warrant 50A by part of a warrant for 200A #7547, which issued to John Callaghan the 27 Dec 1823, who assigned part of the same to James Knox, who assigned 50A of the same to Charles Callaghan 25A by part of a warrant for 200A #7466, which issued to James Knox the 15May 1823, who assigned 25A of the same to said Charles Callaghan. The residue (25A) by part of a warrant for 125A #7270 which issued to James Knox, 4 Jun 1822, who assigned 25A of the same to said Callaghan for which said several reasons the said Charles Callaghan claims better right to the said land then the said Samuel Brown and Abraham Bishop have, pursuant to the law in such case made and provided....Alleghany Co. to wit: this day Charles Callaghan personally appeared before me John Callaghan a justice of the peace in and for the Co. aforesaid, and made oath that the within caveat is real and bon-a-fide, made with an intention of procurring the said land for himself in whose name the caveat is entered and not in trust for the benefit of the person against who the caveat is entered, of for the benefit of any other person or persons whosoever except himself. Given under my hand this 14Apr 1825...John Callaghan...Land Office 23 Apr 1825, a copy from the original...Teste William Selden, Reg. Land Office.

1:155 - THIS INDENTURE - 21 Feb 1825 - Michael Mallow, Christina wife to George Mallow his son both of Alleghany Co., a gift of 2 tracts containing 170A on Potts Creek, first 124A by land where George now lives, second 46A adjoining the tract where George now lives...neighbors - Samuel Carpenter...Michael Mallow, no signature for wife. Rec'd 21 Feb 1825 Oliver Callaghan. Delivered to Hale Collins attorney 3 Sept 1941.

1:156 - 28 Dec 1824 - John Graf of Alleghany Co. debtor, Robert McClintic of Bath Co. truste, and Moses McClintic of Bath Co. creditor. Moses is security of John Graf and Peter Graf to Elizabeth Thompson for rent of land where John and Peter reside. Purpose of indemmifying Moses, $1 paid by Robert in trust, misc. farm animals, and household items...John Graf, Robert McClintic, Moses McClintic...witness - Benjamin F. Steele, James Furwell, George Rodgers. Rec'd 21 Feb 1825 Oliver Callaghan.

THIS INDENTURE - 23 Feb 1825 - Francis Foster, Nancy wife to William Callaghan both of Alleghany Co., $1 for 12A on Jackson's River, part of a survey granted Leonard Buzzard, patent of 14A 6 Jul 1812. Conveyed by Leonard and wife Hannah to Foster 22 Sept 1821, recorded 8 May 1822, containing 12A...neighbor - Robinson...Francis Foster, Nancy (X) Foster. Rec'd 23 Feb 1825 Oliver Callaghan.

1:157 - THIS INDENTURE - 13 May 1825 - James Merry, Mary wife to Alleghany Co. and Thomas Karnes of Greenbrier Co., $1 for lot #21, in Covington 1/4A...James Merry, Mary R. Merry. Rec'd 14 May 1825 Oliver Callaghan.

THIS INDENTURE - 20 Feb 1825 - John Wright, Catherine wife to James Gilliland both of Alleghany Co., $500 for 92A by survey 26 Dec 18? on Potts Creek. Patent bearing date 16 Oct 1825 recorded in Botetourt Co. Also land by deed executed by William Scott to said Wright 10 Oct 1793 recorded in Botetourt Co. on Potts Creek joining the above patent of 92A and contains 42A...neighbors - Eve Johnston,

Linkhorns, and Christopher Persinger...John Wright, Catherine (X) Wright...release of dower by John Persinger and John Arritt 28 Feb 1825. Rec'd Oliver Callaghan. Lifted by Joseph Damron.

1:159 - THIS INDENTURE - 9 Mar 1825 - David Holly of Alleghany Co. to John A. Reed of Greenbrier Co., $5 for 50A in Alleghany Co. on Oglies Creek...neighbors - John Arritt, and James Knox...David Holly. Rec'd 11 Mar 1825 Oliver Callaghan. Lifted by John A. Reid 19 Oct 1830.

1:160 - 17 Sept 1823 - John McCausland, _ wife of Bath Co.debtor, William McClung creditor, and Charles L. Francisco trustee. John and wife to secure payment for debts of $530 for William McClung placed in trust to Charles, 2 tracts located Cow Pasture in Bath Co. The first tract of 125A granted to John Putnam assignee of Andrew Lewis patent 8 Nov 1797. Second tract 100A granted William Gillaspie patent 15 Nov 1798...neighbors - Donnally and Graham...John McCausland, Charles L. Francisco...witness - Walter Richards, William Kincaid, Alex McPhillip, Samuel Lewis. *One other tract being one which John now lives on which he purchased from William Gillespie, also 1 negro boy named Wood...John McCausland, Charles L. Francisco...Ack'd in Bath Co. 14 Oct 1823, H. M. Moffett. Rec'd Mar 1825 Oliver Callaghan.

1:162 - 22 Mar 1825 - William McCallister debtor to William H. Terrill trustee, both of Alleghany Co. William McCallister indebted to James Merry creditor, executed by McCallister to the firm of Richard Smith which was transfered to James Merry as one of the partners of the firm. One note dated 20 Mar 1820 for $66.86 secured by sum of $133.73 subject to 2 credits, $12.10 paid Dec 1821 and $2 paid 1 Jan 1822. The other obligation of $5.44, 10 Jan 1821. Placed in trust to William H. Terrill is misc farm animals...William (X) McCallister, William H. Terrill. Rec'd Mar 1825 Oliver Callaghan. Lifted by William Terrill Aug 1828.

1:163 - THIS INDENTURE - 21 Mar 1825 - Jacob Persinger to William Humphries, both of Alleghany Co., $20 for 284A on Blue Spring Run. Part of a tract of 924A granted to Jacob Persinger 9 Oct 1798...Jacob

Persinger. Rec'd Apr 1825 Oliver Callaghan. Lifted by Jessie Humphries 15 Nov 1830.

1:164 - Bond of $2,000 posted by John Callaghan, Joseph Damron, David Hank, and Isaac Steel. The condition is such that John Callaghan is appointed guardian of Lucy Kean...John Callaghan, Joseph Damron, David Hank, Isaac Steel.

THIS INDENTURE - 4 Apr 1825 - Andrew Beime, George Beime Polly wife of Monroe Co. to George Sawyer of Alleghany Co., $1 for 50A on Dunlap's Creek. Conveyed to Andrew by John Hawkins, 8 Jul 1814, recorded in Monroe Co...neighbors - Sampson Sawyer's heirs...Andrew Beime, George Beime, Polly Beime...Ack'd 4 Apr 1825 by Isaac Hutchinson, clerk Monroe Co...release of dower in Monroe Co. by James Handley and Robert Coalter. Rec'd May 1825 Oliver Callaghan.

1:165 - 6 Apr 1825 - George Sawyer, Rachael wife debtor, John Callaghan Oliver Callaghan trustees, both of Alleghany Co., and Andrew, George, Andrew Jr. Beime of Monroe Co. creditors. George Sawyer indebted to the Beimes $600 payable 23 Mar 1827, also $628.25 payable before 23 Mar 1827. Placed in trust for $1 to John and Oliver 2 tracts in Alleghany Co. on Dunlaps Creek, first 71A which was purchased by George Sawyer from his father which was decreed to be sold by Chancelor of Lewisburg on 10 Jun 1824 for benfit of Andrew Sawyer executor of Sampson Sawyer dec'd, executed by George Sawyer with deed of trust to James Merry and William Terrill 25 Sept 1824. Second tract 30A joining land of Sampson Sawyer dec'd was conveyed to George Sawyer from Andrew and George Beime 14 Apr 1825...George Sawyer, Rachael Sawyer, John Callaghan, Oliver Callaghan...released of dower by Charles Callaghan, and Sampson Sawyer. Rec'd May 1825 Oliver Callaghan. Lifted by John J. McMahon 12 Jun 1828.

1:167 - 7 May 1824 - Hazel Williams, Nancy wife of Greenbrier Co. to James Merry and William H. Terrill. Hazel to secure payment owed by him and George Reader, George Retowell and William H. Morgon and partner in Lynchburg, $1,793, 1 Sept 1824. Placed in trust for $1 to James Merry and William Terrill 3 tracts in Alleghany Co., 117A, 13A,

140A. Land was conveyed to Hazel and Elisha Williams by Moses H. Mann trustee for George Sively 6 May 1820, executed by Archibald Morris and Elizabeth his wife 12 Apr 1823...Hazel Williams, Nancy Williams, James Merry, William H. Terrill...Acknowledged in Greenbrier Co. by James Frazer and James Mclaughlin...Release of dower in Greenbrier Co. by Francis Ludington and Addison Frazer, 9 May 1825. Recorded May 1825 Oliver Callaghan.

1:170 - Bond of $2,000 put up by John Crow, Bernard Pitzer, and Andrew Sawyer to Peter Pence, Sampson Sawyer, Moses H. Mann and Isaac Steel, justices of Alleghany Co. The condition is such that John Crow is appointed guardian to Samuel Brown Jr...John Crow, Barnard Pitzer, Andrew Sawyer...Teste Oliver Callaghan.

16 May 1825 - Bond of $1,000 put up by James Kindell and David Lockhart to the President and Directors of James River Company. The condition is such that James Kindell has agreed with William Anderson, Comissioner of Kanawha Road and Navigation to keep toll gate on road near Callaghans, and to collect the tolls...James Kindell, David Lockhart...Teste Oliver Callaghan.

THIS INDENTURE - 20 Jun 1825 - James McCallister to Daniel Miller, both of Alleghany Co., $150 for 200A on Dunlaps Creek, survey date 28 Mar 1793...James McCallister. Rec'd Jun 1825 Oliver Callaghan.

1:171 - 22 Jun 1825 - William Herbert debtor of Alleghany Co. to Johnson Reynolds trustee of Greenbrier Co. William to secure payment of $72 with interest from 1 Nov 1821 to Oliver Callaghan creditor (by judgement) placed in trust for $1 to Johnson a negro girl named Mariah, 16 yrs...William Herbert, Johnson Reynolds...Teste Oliver Callaghan.

1:173 - THIS INDENTURE - 14 Jun 1825 - William Johnson executor of last will and testament of John Johnson dec'd of Gallia Co. OH, as well Hyriam Johnson of Mason Co. VA who is joint executor. The executors of the first part to William Matheny of Alleghany Co. of the second part, $1 paid by Matheny for a parcel of land in Rich patch on Karne's Run formely called Wooley's Run, part of a survey of 1,000A granted John by patant 13 Sept 1796 joining Mathenys tract of 100A...William Johnson. Rec'd Jun 1825 Oliver Callaghan.

1:174 - 18 Jul 1825 - James B. Littlepage debtor of Alleghany Co. to Johnson Reynolds trustee of Greenbrier Co. James indebted to William Littlepage creditor of Greenbrier Co. in the sum of $178.39 with interest on $56.35 from 22 Sept 1821, with like in trust on $122.03 the residue from 27 Feb 1823 till paid. Placed in trust for $1 to Johnson house and lot in Covington adjoining James Karnes. Lot purchased by James from Thomas Byrd, lot # _ James B. Littllepage, Johnson Reynolds. Rec'd Oliver Callaghan.

1:175 - THIS INDENTURE - 14 Jul 1825 - James Merry, Mary R. wife to Joseph Stillings both of Alleghany Co., $1 for lot # 108 in Covington 1/4A. Lot was first purchased by James Karnes at the public sale of lot by Merry and deeded to Stillings at the request of Karnes...James Merry, Mary R. Merry. Rec'd Aug 1825 Oliver Callaghan.

1:176 - THIS INDENTURE - 1 Sept 1825 - Felix G. Hansford, Sarah wife of Greenbrier Co. to, William Scott and William Kyle, merchants and partners under the firm of Scott and Kyle of Covington. $550 for lot in Covington opposit the Courthouse, between lots of William H. Terrill and Oliver Callaghan, # 88...Felix G. Hansford, Sarah K. Hansford...release of dower by James Frazer and William Spotts in Greenbrier Co. Rec'd Sept 1825 Oliver Callaghan.

1:177 - THIS INDENTURE - 10 Aug 1825 - William Johnston, Susannah wife to Isaac Wolf both of Alleghnay Co., $200 for 69A on Blue Spr Run. First granted by patent 20 Sept 1793 to Eve Johnston now dec'd and by her will conveyed to William Johnston...William Johnston, Susanna Johnston...releases of dower by Michael Arritt and John Arritt. Rec'd Sept 1825 Oliver Callaghan.

1:178 - THIS INDENTURE - _ Aug 1825 - William Johnston, Susanna wife to Jacob Wolf both of Alleghany Co., $100 for 36A located on Potts Creek in Rich Patch on Blue Spring Run, first patented 2 May 1825 to William Johnston...William Johnston, Susanna Johnston...release of dower by Michael Arritt and John Arritt 10 Aug 1825. Rec'd Sept 1825 Oliver Callaghan.

1:179 - 19 Sept 1825 - Bond of $1,000 by Patrick Millhollin, George Mallow and Conrad Fudge to the Governor, James Pleasants of VA. The condition is such that Patrick Millhollin has been appointed Commissioner of Public Relation for 1826...Patrick Millhollin, George Mallow, Conrad Fudge. Rec'd Oliver Callaghan.

1:180 - 14 Jul 1825 - George Sawyer, Rachael wife of Alleghany Co. debtor, James Merry and William Scott trustee, Andrew and George Beime of Monroe Co., creditor. George Sawyer stands indebted to Andrew and George Beime for $335.50 payable in 2 notes, 1 for $135.50 and the other for $200. James Merry and William Scott paid $1 to George and Rachael for 5 tracts of land in Alleghany Co. First tract contains 100A on Dunlaps Creek which was conveyed to George Meyers by Robert Anderson, 10 May 1820 recorded in Botetourt Co. The second tract of 120A on Dunlaps Creek adjoining the lands of Alexander Nelson on the sourthside. The third tract of 100A on Dunlaps Creek conveyed to George Sawyer by William Sawyer adjoining tract of George Sawyers own land of 71A which he purchased from his father Sampson Sawyer recorded in Botetourt Co. The fourth tract contains 170A on Peter's Mt. adjoining the big survey conveyed to George Sawyer by Henry Nicholas recorded in Botetourt Co. The fifth tract 30A patent on Dunlaps Creek adjoining John Hardy and the tract of 100A which was deeded to George Sawyer by Robert Anderson along with misc. personal property...George Sawyer, James Merry, William Scott...Recorded Monroe Co 14 Jul 1825, James Hanley, Robert Coalter. Rec'd Sept 1825 Oliver Callaghan. Lifted by John J. ? was ? Jun 1828.

1:182 - 14 Oct 1825 - Alexander McClintic, heir and legal representive of William McClintic dec'd to, Robert Thomas, Moses McClintic and Alexander H. McClintic all of Bath Co., $1 for 240A which was granted to William McClintic dec'd and decended to Alexander. Land on both sides of Roberts Run, branch of Jackson River...Alexander McClintic...witness - Robert Kincade, Archibald M. Kincade, Samuel McKinsey. Rec'd 15 Oct 1825 Oliver Callaghan.

1:183 - 21 Nov 1825 - Bond of $1,000 by William Callaghan, Joseph Damron, William H. Terrill, and Henry Smith to the Governor of VA. Condition is as such that William Callaghan is appointed Commissioner of Public Revenue...William Callaghan, Joseph Damron, William H. Terrill, Henry Smith. Rec'd Nov 1825 Oliver Callaghan.

20 Mar 1825 - Bond of $1,000 by Charles Callaghan, Jessie Davis and John Persinger to the President and Directors of the Literary Fund. Condition is as such that Charles Callaghan is appointed Treasurer for the year ending 21 Nov 1826...Charles Callaghan, Jessie Davis, John Persinger. Rec'd Nov 1825 Oliver Callaghan.

1:184 - 28 Oct 1825 - John Neal Sr. dec'd of Alleghany Co. during his lifetime made a will whereas he directed the sale of his land and estate and appointed Col. John Crow executor, who refused, so Joseph Damron administered on said dec'ds estate with the will annexed. Joseph Damron admin. of John Neal Sr. to Alice Neal, Polly Neal, and Rebecca Neal $875 paid to Joseph paid $125 to secure land on Dunlaps Creek adjoining John Damron, 220A part granted to Robert Eastham patent 1 Jun 1784 then conveyed to John Neal Sr., 20 1/2A was conveyed to John Neal by Samuel McMullin, 25 Mar 1807, and 9 A was granted to John Neal patent 11 May 1795, all together 249 1/2A...neighbor - General Lewis...Joseph Damron, with will annexed of John Neal Sr...witness - James McCallister, Samuel McCallister, Hugh N. Neal and Cornelius Vanstavern. Rec'd Nov 1825 Oliver Callaghan.

1:186 - 21 Nov 1825 -Bond of Joseph Damron, Samuel Kean, Charles Callaghan, Andrew Sawyer, David Lockhart, Andrew Persinger, and George Sively unto Governor James Pleasants Esq. in the amount of $3,000. The condition is as such that Joseph Damron is appointed surveyor in place of William Herbert dec'd...Joseph Damron, Samuel Kean, Charles Callaghan, Andrew Sawyer, David Lockhart, Andrew Persinger, George Sively. Rec'd 21 Nov 1825 Oliver Callaghan.

THIS INDENTURE - 2 Dec 1825 - William Hite, Rachael wife to James Merry, $1 for 2 tracts on Jacksons River. First tract deeded to William Hite by Benjamin Haynes, second tract deeded to William Hite by Jacob Butcher...neighbor - Alexander Blair...William Hite, Rachael Hite. Rec'd 5 Dec 1825 Oliver Callaghan.

1:187 - 30 Mar 1825 - George Rayhill of St. Clair Co. IL appoints Dr. James Merry of Alleghany Co. his lawful attorney to sue and recover from the estate of D. Kean dec'd...George Rayhill...Witness - R. M. Chandler, John Thomas Jr...Ack'd at Bellville in St. Clair Co. 30 Mar 1825 Able Fike, John Hay, Samuel M. Roberts. Rec'd Dec 1825 by request of Nicholas Vanstavern, Oliver Callaghan.

16 Jan 1826 - Thomas Richardson and John Richardson are bound to John L. Boswell, Charles Callaghan, Robert Kincaid and Sampson Sawyer in the amount of $300. The condition is as such that Thomas Richardson is appointed guardian, 14 Oct 1822, to Sally Dressler, Peter Dressler, Henry Dressler, and Malinda Dressler, with William Richardson and Adam Dressler his securties and being ruled by said William Richardson to give counter security hath tendered the above bond with the said John Richardson as his security. At court 16 Jan 1826 court exonerated William Richardson from his securityship in the aforesaid bond and received in his stead the said John Richardson as security in this bond in guardianship of Thomas Richardson in guardianship of the infant children of Charles Dressler dec'd. Sally and Peter now being of lawful age...Thomas Richardson, John Richardson. Rec'd Jan 1826 Oliver Callaghan.

1:189 - 10 Jan 1826 - Isaac Steel, Julia wife of Alleghany Co. to Hugh P. Taylor of the city of Richmond, paid $1,000 for lot # 90 in Covington located on Third St...Isaac Steel, Julia Steel...release of dower by Sampson Sawyer, and John Callaghan. Rec'd Jan 1826 Oliver Callaghan. Lifted by H. P. Taylor 9 Apr 1828.

1:190 - 25 Nov 1825 - Bond of Nancy Kimberline and William Kimberline to Joseph D. Keyser, John L. Boswell, Michael Arritt, Robert Kincaid and JohnArritt in the amount of $3,000 . Condition is such that Nancy is appointed guardian to Elizabeth Ann Kimberline, Washington Kimberline, Lorezo D. Kimberline, Nancy Kimberline infants of James Kimberline on 19 May 1823. With John Callaghan, Oliver Callaghan, Dennison Rose, and Thomas Byrd, her securities, and ruled by Dennison Rose to give counter security with leave for Nancy to enter into another bond with William Kimberline...Nancy Kimberline, William Kimberline. Rec'd 19 Dec 1825 Oliver Callaghan.

1:191 - THIS INDENTURE - 14 Dec 1825 - Thomas Kearns, Jane wife of Greenbrier Co. to Hugh Linch of Greenbrier Co., $1 for lot # 21 in

Covington, 1/4A...Thomas Kearns, Jane Kearns...release of dower by Robert Stephen and Henry Erskine of Greenbrier Co. 11 Dec 1825. Rec'd Jan 1826 Oliver Callaghan.

1:192 - THIS INDENTURE - 14 Jan 1826 - William Matheny, Jane wife to Rebecca Matheny both of Alleghany Co., $100 for 2 tracts in Richpatch. One tract part of 100A granted William Matheny patent 29 Sept 1823, joining the parcel of land William Matheny bought from William Johnston executor of John Johnson dec'd and others. Contains 28A, neighbors - George Steel and Shoemaker. Second tract part of 1,000A granted John Johnson dec'd patent ?, conveyed to William Matheny from William Johnston 14 Jun 1825 containing 17A...William Matheny, Jane (X) Matheny...release of dower by Peter Pence, and Stephen Hooks 14 Jan 1826. Rec'd Feb 1826 Oliver Callaghan.

1:194 - THIS INDENTURE - 14 Jan 1826 - William Matheny, Jane wife to William Shoemaker of Botetourt Co., for $100 paid $1 now for land in Richpatch joining land of Thomas Davis, purchased from John Johnson's representatives containing 72A part of survey of 100A granted to William Matheny patent 29 Sept 1823...William Matheny, Jane (X) Matheny...release of dower by Stephen Hook and Peter Pence 14 Jan 1826. Rec'd Feb 1826 Oliver Callaghan.

1:195 - THIS INDENTURE - 10 Feb 1826 - Isaac Steel, Julia wife to Hugh Taylor, $200 for lots # 113 & 114 in Covington on Third St., each 1/4A. Deeded to Isaac by James Merry and wife...Isaac Steel, Julia Steel...Release of dower Charles and John Callaghan 10 Feb 1826. Rec'd Feb 1826 Oliver Callaghan.

THIS INDENTURE - 11 Jul 1825 - James Breckenridge of Botetourt Co. to Henry Smith, Alexander Wilson, Rebecca wife 450A on Gillespies Mill Creek in trust for the purpose of securing payment of a debt appearing in Botetourt Co. court 24 Aug 1810. Said land was sold by James Breckinridge as trustee. Part of property came to Nicholas Vanstavern who before he obtained a deed made sale to Henry Smith to whom he directed a title be made first. Survey 28 Nov 1819, $750 paid by Nicholas Vanstavern to Henry Smith original sum contracted receipt held by James Breckenridge as trustee of aforesaid, sells to

Henry Smith land containing 55A...James Breckenridge...Rec'd in Botetourt Co. July 1825, H. W. Bowyer. Rec'd Feb 1826 Oliver Callaghan.

1:198 - THIS INDENTURE - 16 Apr 1825 - John Delorn, Catherine wife to Samuel Kean, $100 for 50A on Snake Run, joining the land of George Carson dec'd, part of 150A patent to Delorn 26 Sept 1823... John Delorn, Catherine Delorn...release of dower Oliver Callaghan. Rec'd Apr 1825 Oliver Callaghan.

1:199 - THIS INDENTURE - 17 Mar 1826 - Peter Pence, Elizabeth wife to Michael Vincent, both of Alleghany Co., $1 for lot # 89 in Covington 1/4A...Peter Pence, Betsy Pence. Rec'd 17 Mar 1826 Oliver Callaghan.

1:201 - THIS INDENTURE - 15 Mar 1826 - William H. Terrill, James Merry trustees, George Sawyer debtor, and Andrew Sawyer executor of Sampson Sawyer dec'd creditor. George on 25 Sept 1824 to secured payment of $450.80, also to secure payment of $? to Andrew Sawyer did by indenture of trust convey to William H. Terrill and James Merry the following property to wit; land on Dunlaps Creek which George claimed by purchase from his father, which was to be sold by the Chancellor of Lewisburg on ? Jun 1824, 70A...William H. Terrill, James Merry, Andrew Sawyer. Rec'd 15 Mar 1826 Oliver Callaghan.

1:202 - THIS INDENTURE - 2 Mar 1826 - Michael Vincent purchased lots # 83 & 84 from James and Samuel Merry Aug 1818, he lost his deed certificate. Michael sold lots to Oliver Callaghan. James Merry will re-deed lots to Oliver...James Merry, Mary R. Merry...release of dower by Isaac Steel and John L. Boswell. Rec'd Mar 1826 Oliver Callaghan.

1:205 - THIS INDENTURE - 18 Mar 1826 - Archibald Armstrong of Greenbrier Co. to Benjamin Thompson of Bath Co., $1 for all right and title and interest in land lying in Bath Co. and Alleghany Co., patent to Robert Armstrong Jr. on Jackson River adjoining Benjamin Thomspon dec'd and Alexander McClintic, Hylsey, Cavendish, John Bollar and Jacob Painturf. It decended to Archibald from his borther-in-law and sister, James Steel and Elizabeth Steel...Archibald Armstrong...Rec'd 18 Mar 1826 in Greenbrier Co., Thomas Kirkpatrick, and James Kincaid. Rec'd Mar 1826 Oliver Callaghan.

THIS INDENTURE - 22 Jul 1826 - Thomas Byrd, Dianah wife of Bath Co. to Joseph Stillings of Alleghany Co., $100 for lot # 81 on Third St. in Covington, 1/4A...Thomas Byrd, Dianna Byrd...Randolph Co. recorded by Robert McCrumb and George Weeks...release of dower in Bath Co. by William McDean and William McClintic. Rec'd Oct 1826 Oliver Callaghan.

1:207- THIS INDENTURE - 25 May 1826 - James Merry, Mary wife to Hazel Williams of Greenbrier Co., $784 for lots # 41 & 42, 64, 65 & 66 in Covington, 1/4A each...James Merry, Mary Merry. Rec'd Jun 1826 Oliver Callaghan.

1:208 - Valentine Jones deeded to David Kean (who is dec'd) land surveyed for Henry Bailey Greenwood 7 Jun 1785 on Dunlaps Creek. Kean died intestate before Jones could make deed containing 100A which Kean left to his heirs, Samuel and Lucy Kean. THIS INDENTURE - 22 Apr 1825 - Samuel Kean, Lucy wife to Valentine Jones, Loviah wife, $50 for land located on Jerrys Run, first owned by Edward McMullin and now held by David Kean's heirs and Joseph Crow. Survey containing 180A, Greenwood obtained patent which was supposed to contain 100A. The tract was conveyed to Jones by deed from Henry Bailey Greenwood, Nancy wife 28 Sept 1796 and on record at Sweet Springs, 19 Oct 1796. It is strictly understood to be part and only part now intended to be sold, this land is not within the bounds of the land which David Kean and John Crow purchased from Edward McMullin...Valentine (X) Jones, Loviah (X) Jones...witness - John Callaghan, John Crow, C. Vanstavern, John Crow, Jacob Amen...release of dower by John Crow, and John Callaghan. Rec'd Jun 1826 Oliver Callaghan.

1:210 - 5 Jan 1826 - During last year, 1825, Mr. John Byrd Sr. of Bath Co. whose daughter Elizabeth is my wife sent a negro girl named Prudence to my house for his daughter. I sold the girl for $300, I agreed to replace her with a younger girl Rachel and child named Mary Jane just beginning to talk, for the benfit of her son Benjamin T. B.

Crutchfield. John Byrd Sr. was not happy so I would like to pay $300 and give Rachel and Mary Jane to John Byrd Sr...Francis Crutchfield. Rec'd Jun 1826 Oliver Callaghan.

1:211 - THIS INDENTURE - Francis Crutchfield for love and affection to son John M. D. Crutchfield for $1, 100A being 1/3 part of tract owned by me lying in Alleghany Co. Tract of 300A surveyed in 1802 by John Walker when it was first located in Bath Co...Francis Crutchfield...*the forgoing deed of gift is not to be considered any part of my estate upon my death...Francis Crutchfield. Rec'd Jun 1826 Oliver Callaghan.

THIS INDENTURE - 10 Jan 1826 - John Byrd Sr. of Bath Co. for love and affection I bear Benjamin T. B. Crutchfield, my grandson and in consideration of $1 paid by his father Francis Crutchfield, one small negro girl named Rachel and negro child just begining to talk named Mary Jane formly property of Francis Crutchfield. It is to be understood that the mother Elizabeth, daughter of John Byrd Sr. is to have benefit of said Rachel and Mary Jane during her natural life...John (X) Byrd Sr...Ack'd in Bath Co, 10 Jan 1824, John Slown, Thomas Mullhollin. Rec'd Jun 1826 Oliver Callaghan. Lifted by A. Crutchfield 1830.

1:212 - THIS INDENTURE - 19 Jun 1826 - Michael Mallow, Christina wife to William F. Morton, both of Alleghany Co., $1 paid for 170A lying in bend of Jackson River...neighbors - Conrad Fudge, Henry Dressler dec'd, George Chambers, George Harmon, John Brunnemer...Michael Mallow, no signature for Christina. Rec'd Jun 1826 Oliver Callaghan.

1:214 - 15 Mar 1826 - William H. Terrill and James Merry first part, George Sawyer second part and Andrew Sawyer executor of Sampson Sawyer dec'd third part. George on 25 Sept 1924 to secure payment of $450.80 and $100 to Andrew Sawyer executor of Sampson did by indenture of trust convey to Terrill and Merry the following property, in Alleghany Co. on Dunlaps Creek, a tract of land which George claimed by purchase from his father which was decreed to be sold by Chancellor of Lewisburg, Chancery district on 10 Jun 1824 for the benfit of Andrew Sawyer executor. It was exonerated on conditions, a article of agreement by George and Andrew in the hands of Merry. The tract is estimated to contain 70A. George paid his debts to Andrew, $1 paid by George to Terrill and Merry to release land...William Terrill, James Merry, Andrew Sawyer. Rec'd 15 Mar 1826 Oliver Callaghan.

1:215 - 14 Jan 1826 - John A. North first part, John H. Peyton of Augusta Co. second part. A decree of superior court of Chancery in Greenbrier Co. at the Nov term 1825 depending between John H. Peyton plaintiff and Sarah Mann widow of Hamilton Mann, Lewis Mann, Archibald Mann, John Mann and other children and devises of Moses Mann dec'd of Alleghany Co. were defendents. John A. North appointed commissioner to convey to Peyton title and interest of Hamilton, Lewis, Archibald, John, children and devisers of Moses Mann and Sarah widow of Moses Mann. Land is 43A, 3 rods, and 12 poles, part of mill tract of Moses Mann and joining John Mann, John H. Peyton. Peyton paid $37.50 to North, the amount ascertained by decree. Land located near Falling Spr Run...neighbor George Sively...John A. North...Ack'd in Augusta by John Wayt and John C. Sowers 14 Jan 1826. Rec'd Mar 1826 Oliver Callaghan.

1:217 - 9 Jun 1826 - Mark H. Goshen purchased 2 lots # 31 & 32 in Covington at public sale, 1818, from James Merry. Goshen transfered deed to Michael Vincent and ordered Merry to make deed to Vincent. Vincent sold lots to Isaac Steel, deeds made to Vincent have been lost. Merry agreed to make deed to Steel...THIS INDENTURE - James Merry, Mary wife to Isaac Steel for $282 for 2 lots # 31 & 32 in Covington 1/4/A each...James Merry, Mary Merry. Rec'd Jun 1826 Oliver Callaghan. Lifted by I. Steel 12 Apr 1833.

1:218 - THIS INDENTURE - 24 Feb 1826 - William Mann of Alleghany Co. to Andrew Kincaid, Andrew Sawyer, Samuel Brown, Alleghany Co., John A. Holly of Greenbrier Co., $1 for lots # 43 & 44 in Covington, 1/4A each...William Mann. Rec'd Jun 1826 Oliver Callaghan.

1:219 - THIS INDENTURE - 26 Jan 1826 - William Elliot, Isabella wife of Jackson Co. OH. to Jane Jackson, William Morris, Richard Morris, Nancy Richardson, John Morris, Margaret Keyser, Elizabeth Lockhart,

Ann Morris, Benjamin Morris, children, heirs and representatives of William Morris dec'd of Alleghany Co. Richard Morris the elder departed this life intestate sized and possesed in fee simple several tracts of land in Alleghany Co. William Morris and Isabella Elliott became intitled with other children to equal shares. William Morris by purchase became entitled to interest or shares of Isabella in tracts. He intitled to 2 shares by virtue of decree of Chancery Court at Stanton. William Morris assigned lot #3, share for himself and Isabella Elliot. THIS INDENTURE - William Morris, Isabella wife to parties of second part for $1 134A land...William Elliot, Isabella (X) Elliot...Teste Vincent Southand, David Richmond...release of dower in Jackson Co. OH by Vincent Southand and Thomas Daughtry 26 Jan 1826. Rec'd in Jackson Co. by A. M. Faulkner. Rec'd Jan 1826 Oliver Callaghan. Lifted by A. M. Kincaid 21 Jan 1828.

1:221 - 30 May 1826 - Mark H. Goshen purchased lot in Covington at public sale in 1818, lot # 22. Goshen transferred title to Michael Vincent and ordered James Merry to make deed to Vincent. Vincent transfered title to Robert Bratton. THIS INDENTURE - James Merry, Mary wife to Robert Bratton for $120 lot # 22 in Covington, 1/4A...James Merry, Mary R. Merry. Rec'd 31 May 1826 Oliver Callaghan. Lifted by Robert Bratton 1 Apr 1828.

1:222 - THIS INDENTURE - 29 Dec 1825 - John Rees of Gallia Co. OH to John Hardy of Alleghany Co., $53 for 61A on Dunlaps Creek, land granted 27 Sept 1796 to Samuel Logue and conveyed to John Rees...neighbor - William Snead...John Rees...witness - George Sawyer, Joseph Damron, Cornelius Vanstavern, Francis Foster. Rec'd Jan 1826 Oliver Callaghan.

THIS INDENTURE - 14 Apr 1826 - Abraham Sibert, Jane wife of Ross Co. OH to Phillip Rogers of Alleghany Co., $100 paid for 100A land...neighbors - heirs of John Lewis, Vanlentine Jones...Abraham Sibert, Jane (X) Sibert...witness - W. McDonald, I. Scott...release of dower in Ross Co. by George Johnston and Hiram N. Mead 4 Apr 1826...Rec'd and cert'd in Ross Co. by Humphrey Fullerton and James M. Clintuk. Rec'd Jun 1826 Oliver Callaghan.

1:225 - 28 Mar 1826 - William Patterson debtor, Oliver Callaghan trustee, and John Brunnemer Jr. creditor. William is indebted to John Brunnemer Jr. for $140 in consideration of a bond assigned by John B. to William Patterson on William G. Holloway. Oliver Callaghan paid $1 to William for 205A in Rich Patch...neighbor - Kimberline, Joseph Gramer...William Patterson, Oliver Callaghan, John Brunnemer Jr. Rec'd Mar 1826 Oliver Callaghan.

1:228 - THIS INDENTURE - 3 Feb 1826 - Frederick Armentrout, Elizabeth wife to Jacob Armentrout, both of Allehgany Co., $20 paid for 120A located on Potts Creek, part of a tract deeded by Samuel Davis heirs, to Armentrout...neighbor - William Dew...Frederick (X) Armentrout, Elizabeth (X) Armentrout...witness - Michael Arritt, and John Arritt...release of dower by John and Michael Arritt 3 Feb 1826. Rec'd Apr 1826 Oliver Callaghan.

1:229 - THIS INDENTURE - 6 Mar 1826 - Michael Kimberline for love and affection and $1 to my daughter Maria Kimberline, 2 negros, 1 female about 25 yrs named Charlotte and a child about 4 yrs named Ama...Michael Kimberline...witness - Stephen Hooks, William G. Peter. Rec'd Mar 1826 Oliver Callaghan.

THIS INDENTURE - 19 Feb 1826 - Jacob Wolf, Mary wife to Sampson Persinger both of Alleghany Co., $100 for 70A on Blue Spr Run, part of a tract of 169A patent 5 Nov 1799 to George Faught, conveyed to John Faught then to Jacob Wolf...neighbors - Jacob Persinger, John Faught...Jacob Wolf, Mary (X) Wolf...witness - Michael Arritt and John Arritt...release of dower by John and Michael Arritt 9 Feb 1826. Rec'd Mar 1826 Oliver Callaghan.

1:232 - 6 Mar 1826 - Michael Kimberline for love and affection and $1 to my son Joseph 2 negro girls, one named Elly about 10 yrs and one named Nancy about 3 yrs...Michael Kimberline...witness - Stephen Hooks, William G. Peter. Rec'd Mar 1826 Oliver Callaghan.

29 Oct 1825 - Rebecca Neal debtor, Samuel Kean trustee, and Joseph Damron administrator with will annexed of John Neal creditor. Rebecca indebted to Joseph Damron admin. in sum of $125 by bond dated 20 Oct 1825. Samuel paid $1 to Rebecca for 1 undivided 4th

part of tract which John Neal Sr. dec'd resided on. Land located on Dunlaps Creek joining John Damron and Lewis. The whole tract contains 249 1/2A...Rebecca Neal, Samuel Kean, Joseph Damron...witness - James McCallister, Cornelius Vanstavern, Samuel McCallister, and Hugh Neal. Rec'd Jun 1826 Oliver Callaghan. Lifted by Joseph Damron 20 Oct 1831

1:235 - 14 Mar 1826 - Andrew Sillington of Bath Co. to Ann B. Sillington, Alexander Sillington, John M. Sillington, Mary J. Sillington, Rebecca Sillington, heirs of William Sillington dec'd all of Bath Co. Archibald Morris by indenture dated 19 Dec 1821, recorded in Bath Co., conveyed to Andrew Sillington land on Cedar Creek, land belonging to Andrew Sillington to put up for sale at Millborough. William Sillington bid $360 and purchased. Now Andrew in further execution of trust for $300 sells to the above heirs of William Sillington dec'd...Andrew Sillington...Rec'd Bath Co. by John Slown and William Dean 14 Mar 1826. Rec'd Mar 1826 Oliver Callaghan.

1:237 - THIS INDENTURE - 1 Jul 1826 - Hazel Williams, Nancy wife of Greenbrier Co. to William Burd of the town of Lynchburg, $1 for lot # 64 in Covington adjoining the public square, 1/4A...Hazel Williams, Nancy Williams...release of dower in Greenbrier Co. by David Bright, and Addison Frazer 10 Jul 1821. Rec'd Jul 1826 Oliver Callaghan.

1:239 - THIS INDENTURE - 24 Feb 1819 - James Merry, Mary wife, Samuel Merry to Thomas Byrd both of Botetourt Co., $1 for lots # 81 & 82 in Covington, 1/4A each...James Merry, Mary Merry, Samuel Merry...witness - Richard Smith, D. Callaghan, Benjamin T. Douglas...release of dower by Peter Wright and Joseph D. Keyser of Botetourt Co. 24 Feb 1819. Rec'd 17 Jul 1826 Oliver Callaghan.

1:240 - 9 Sept 1823 - Simon Gillaspie of Montgomery Co. KY administrator of Simon Gillaspie dec'd of VA do appoint James H. Gillaspie of Mongomery Co. KY my attorney to do all business as administrator of Simon Gillaspie dec'd...Simon Gillaspie...Ack'd in Montgomery Co. KY by Mieajah Harrison and John Creason Sept 1823. Rec'd Jul 1826 Oliver Callaghan.

1:241 - THIS INDENTURE - 3 Dec 182? - James H. Gillaspie of Montgomery Co. KY attorney for Simon Gillaspie of aforesaid Co. and state to Thomas Newell of Botetourt Co., $500 for 1 undivided 4th of land in Allaghany Co. on Wilson Creek, patent 1,000A was Simon Gillaspies and on his death decended to his 4 children, John, Simon, Rebecca Wilson, and Nancy Newell, subject to dower...neighbors - John Beal and John Linglangher and Hansbrger...James H. Gillaspie...Ack'd in Botetourt Co. by David Rowland, and E. Sweetland 2 Dec 1825. Rec'd July 182 ? Oliver Callaghan.

1:242 - THIS INDENTURE - 18 Jul 1826 - William F. Morton to Hugh P. Taylor both of Alleghany Co., $80 for lot # 113 in Covington on Back St., 1/4A...Hugh P. Taylor. Rec'd Aug 1826 Oliver Callaghan.

1:243 - THIS INDENTURE - 18 Jul 1826 - Alexander Fleet to Hugh P. Taylor both of Alleghany Co., $100 for lot # 114 in Covington on Third St. 1/4A...Alexander Fleet. Rec'd Aug 1826 Oliver Callaghan.

18 Jul 1826 - Joseph Stillings, Jane wife debtor, Hugh P. Taylor trustee and Oliver Callaghan creditor, all of Alleghany Co. Joseph indebted to Oliver for $78.70 by bond. Joseph and Jane paid $1 by Hugh for Lot # 81 in Covington, 1/4A...Joseph Stillings, Jane Stillings, Hugh P. Taylor, Oliver Callaghan...release of dower 18 Jul 1826 by John L. Boswell and Isaac Steel. Rec'd Aug 1826 Oliver Callaghan. Lifted by H. P. Taylor 15 Feb 1828.

1:246 - 11 Apr 1825 - Being called by Benjamin Haynes, Corneluis Vanstavern, William Snead, to lay off land which Haynes bought from William Smith on Dunlaps Creek by the direction of Capt. Samuel Brown and Samuel Kean Sr. commissioners chosen by the parties for that purpose. All parties present...Joseph Damron...first lot of 43A, 1 rod, 31 poles to Vanstavern, second lot of 52A, 3 rods, 6 poles, to William Snead...Benjamin Haynes, Corneluis Vanstavern, William Snead...witness - Joseph Damron. Rec'd Aug 1826 Oliver Callaghan.

1:248 - THIS INDENTURE - 19 Aug 1826 - George Stull, Jane wife of Alleghany Co. to John Stull of Botetourt Co., $1 for 42A on Karnes Creek granted to George Stull patent 29 Sept 1823...neighbor - John

Johnston...George Stull, Jane (X) Stull...release of dower by Stephen Hooks and Peter Pence. Rec'd Sept 1826 Oliver Callaghan.

1:249 - THIS INDENTURE - 1 May 1826 - James H. Gillaspie, lawful agent of Montgomery Co. KY, to Thomas Newell of Botetourt Co., $500 for one 4th undivided land on Wilsons Creek, 1,000A derived by Simon Gillaspie and Elizabeth wife from the death of his father Simon, subject to widow's dower...neighbors - John Hansbarger, Archibald Linglocker, heirs of John Beal and Boston Shovers heirs...Simon Gillaspie, Elizabeth Gillaspie...Ack'd in Montgomery Co. by Mieajah Harrison and Silas W. Robbins. Rec'd Sept 1826 Oliver Callaghan.

1:251 - 21 Nov 1826 - bond of Charles Callaghan, Jessie Davis, William H. Terrill in the amount of $2,000 to the President and Directors of the Literary Fund. Condition is that Charles Callaghan is appointed Treasure...Charles Callaghan, Jessie Davis, William H. Terrill. Recorded Nov 1826 Oliver Callaghan.

20 Mar 1826 - Denison Rose debtor, James Gilliland trustee, Andrew Persinger creditor. Denison to secure payment of $624.60 due by bond to Lewis ?, $1 paid to Denison by James for misc. household and farm items....Teste - R. Littlepage, Robert Calhoun...Denison Rose, James Gilliland. Rec'd Nov 1826 Oliver Callaghan.

1:252 - 4 Jul 1826 - Surveyed and divided for John Stull and George Stull devises of George Stull Sr. dec'd, land in Rich Patch by patent 100A, by survey 91A orginally granted to Jacob Stull by patent 22 Apr 1805 which ascended from said Jacob upon his decease to his father George Sr. by direction of Stephen Hooks, Jacob Kimberline, and Charles Fridley. George 35A and John 56A...neighbors - Reid...Joseph Damron...Teste - Stephen Hooks and Peter Pence. Rec'd Sept 1826 Oliver Callaghan.

1:256 - THIS INDENTURE - 22 Jul 1826 - Thomas Byrd, Dianah wife of Bath Co. to Joseph Stillings of Alleghany Co., $100 for lot # 81 in Covington on Third St., 1/4A...Thomas Byrd, Dianah Byrd...Randolph Co. SC, deed ack'd by Robert McCrumb and George Weas...realease of dower by William McDean and William McClintic. Rec'd Aug 1826 Oliver Callaghan.

1:257 - THIS INDENTURE - 29 Aug 1826 - Jacob Nicely, Betsy wife to John Jorday of Rockbridge Co., $300 for ?22A...Jacob Nicely, Betsy (X) Nicely...release of dower by Joseph D. Keyser and William H. Haynes 31 Aug 1826. Rec'd Oct 1826 Oliver Callaghan. Lifted by F. Jordan 22 Feb 1831.

1:259 - 18 Sept 1826 - Bond of William Callaghan, John Callaghan, and Joseph Damron to John Taylor Esq., Governor in the amount of $1,000. Condition is as such that William is appointed Commissioner of Public Revenue for the year of 1827...William Callaghan, John Callaghan, Joseph Damron...Teste Oliver Callaghan.

THIS INDENTURE - 23 Oct 1826 - Lasson Brooks, Catharine wife to George Moyer, both of Alleghany Co., $75 paid for one undivided 9th part of a tract containing 134A, part of the estate of George Moyer Sr. dec'd on Dunlaps Creek...Lasson Brooks, Catherine Brooks. Rec'd Oct 1826 Oliver Callaghan.

1:260 - THIS INDENTURE - 10 Jul 1822 - Mathew Wilson, Elizabeth wife of Bedford Co. to Henry Tressler of Alleghany Co., $1 for lot # 87 in Covington on Bath St. 1/4A...Mathew Wilson, Elizabeth Wilson...release of dower in Bedford Co. by William R. Jones and Willian R. Porter 12 Jul 1822. Rec'd Nov 1826 Oliver Callaghan.

1:261 - 21 Nov 1826 - Johnson Reynolds of Greenbrier Co. to William S. Littlepage, a deed of trust executed by James B. Littlepage to secure sum of money in said deed of trust to William Littlepage. Deed is recorded in Alleghany Co., it was given on a house in Covington, house and lot sold on Nov 1826 to William. THIS INDENTURE - Johnson Reynolds to William S. Littlepage for $205 lot and house in Covington on Bath St...neighbor Oliver Callaghan...Johnson Reynolds. Rec'd Nov 1826 Oliver Callaghan.

1:262 - THIS INDENTURE - 1 Apr 1823 - Henry Dressler, Elizabeth wife to Nash Legrand both of Alleghany Co. $1 for lot # 87 in Covington on Bath St. 1/4A...Henry Dressler, Elizabeth Dressler. Rec'd Nov 1 1826 Oliver Callaghan.

11 Sept 1827 - Michael Dressler, Mary wife to Henry Dressler, $1 for their right and title in land left by his father Henry Dressler, also their right and interest to his brother Moses Dressler dec'd...Michael Dressler, Mary Dressler...Ack'd by George Mallow and Samuel B. Lowery. Rec'd Sept 1827 William Holloway.

1:263 - 3 Sept 1826 - William Scott and William Kyle, equal partners, purchased from Felix Hansford and Sarah wife lot # 88 by deed bearing date of 1 Sept 1825 for $550. THIS INDENTURE - William Kyle, Agnes wife to William Scott their undivided half, $1,093...neighbor - William Terrill...William Kyle, Agnes Kyle...release of dower by John L. Boswell and Samuel B. Lowery 3 Sept 1827. Rec'd Sept 1827 Oliver Callaghan. Lifted by William Scott 17 May 1828.

1:265 - 21 Nov 1826 - William Bess and Henry Bess debtor, William A. Terrill trustee, Andrew Fudge and Jacob Fudge creditor. William and Henry indebted to Andrew and Jacob in the sum of $35.70, placed in trust to William A. Terrill for $1, 1 mare and tabacco crop...William (X) Bess, Henry (X) Bess, William H. Terrill. Rec'd 21 Nov 1826 William Holloway.

1:266 - 19 Dec 1826 - Francis Crutchfield first debtor, William H. Terrill, James Merry trustees, George Sively creditor. Francis indebted to George Sively for $134.38, placed in trust for $1, 2 negro girls Patsy and Sally, 16 yrs and 15 yrs...Francis Crutchfield, William H. Terrill, James Merry. Rec'd Jan 1827 William Holloway.

1:267 - THIS INDENTURE - 27 Feb 1827 - Valentine Jones, Loviah wife of Alleghany Co. to Archibald Smith of Monroe Co., $100 for 50A on Snake Run, granted to Vanlentine Jones, patent bearing date of 7 Oct 1813...neighbors - James Brown, William Herbert heirs...Valentine (X) Jones, Loviah Jones...release of dower Sampson Sawyers, Joseph Damron. Rec'd Feb 1827 William Holloway.

1:269 - 12 Nov 1827 - William McCollister Jr., Mary wife to George Moyer, $50 for their right in 2 tracts from her father George Moyers Sr. located on Dunlaps Creek. First tract granted to William Hunter by patent 1 Sept 1781, conveyed by Hunter to David Tate, then by David and Comfort his wife to George Moyer Sr. being recorded in Botetourt

Co. Oct 1790. Second tract granted 1 Jul 1817 for 74A, in all 134A. Williams and Mary share one 9th decesended to Mary as heir of George Moyer Sr...William McCollister, Polly (X) McCollister. Ack'd Oliver Callaghan, rec'd Nov 1827 William Holloway.

1:271 - 18 Sept 1826 - Barbara McCallisters right of dower surveyed by Moses H. Mann, Conrad Fudge, John Boswell and Henry Dressler, commissioners appointed. Widow of John McCallister, received 37A...Joseph Damron. Rec'd Nov 1826 Oliver Callaghan.

1:274 - THIS INDENTURE - 22 Oct 1827 - Cornelius Vanstavern, Agnes wife to John Hardy, $500 for 2 tracts. First one on Dunlap Creek conveyed by William Smith to Benjamin Haynes, then conveyed to Cornelius, recorded Alleghany Co. Oct 1827 containing 51A...neighbors - William Snead, and John Hardy. Second tract 43A neighbors - James Brown...Cornelius Vanstavern, Agnes Vanstavern...release of dower by Sampson Sawyer, and Joseph Damron. Rec'd 17 Nov 1827 William G. Holloway.

1:272 - THIS INDENTURE - 5 Nov 1827 - William McCallister Jr., Mary wife to Andrew Kincaid, $10 for 2 tracts. First tract Andrew is now residing on, Jackson River. Second tract located at Oliver Mt., both containing 206A. Andrew purchased 1 undivided 7th of one 6th of one 7th part and half of land which William McCallister Jr. claims as one 7th heirs of Mary McCallister dec'd formerly Mary Kincaid who intermarried with John McCallister. The interest claim having decended to William McCallister Jr. in consequence of death of his mother Mary. Mary became entitled to one 7th of one 6th of one 7th part of the tracts by death of her brother Thomas Kincaid...William McCallister, Mary (X) McCallister. Ack'd 16 Nov 1827 by Oliver Callaghan, rec'd William Holloway.

1:276 - William McCallister, Mary wife appoint Dr. James Merry their attorney for purpose of exhibiting a bill on the Chancery side of Court on the subject of land and negros which decesended to them and others as heirs of John McCallister dec'd. Land and negros are to be sold and proceeds divided among the several heirs...William McCallister, Mary (X) McCallister...Teste Oliver Callaghan, rec'd 16 Nov 1827 William Holloway.

1:277 - THIS INDENTURE - 25 Jan 1827 - James Merry, Mary R. wife to James Karnes, $60 for lot # 78 in Covington, 1/4A...James Merry, Mary R. Merry...release of dower by Samuel B. Lowery and John L. Boswell. Rec'd Feb 1827 William G. Holloway.

1:279 - THIS INDENTURE - 20 Feb 1827 - James Merry, Mary wife to Thomas Crutchfield, $1 for lot # 79 in Covington on Bath and First St., 1/4A...James Merry, Mary R. Merry...release of dower by subscribing justices of the peace. Rec'd Mar 1927 Oliver Callaghan.

THIS INDENTURE - 11 Nov 1826 - Nash Legrand to William H. Terrill, $1 for lot # 87 in Covington with house...Nash Legrand...Richmond Corp. Ack'd by James Rawlings and A. Pleasants 11 Nov 1827. Rec'd Apr 1827 William Holloway.

1:280 - THIS INDENTURE - 21 Nov 1826 - James Ross, Elizabeth wife formely Elizabeth Griffith, Nancy Griffith, James Clendenen, Sally wife formely Sally Griffith, heirs of William Griffith dec'd of Bath Co. to Orlando Griffith of Bath Co., $27.84 to each of them paid for 3 6th part of tract of 130A in Alleghany Co. on Cowpasture River...James (X) Ross, James Clendenen...witness - Fountain Morrison, Griffith Ross, John Shawer. Rec'd Jun 1827 William Holloway.

1:281 - 19 Mar 1827 - John Richardson for natural love and affection for my son William Richardson and in consideration of $1 paid do give and grant 100A on Jackson River, southeast side of Lick Mt...John Richardson. Rec'd Mar 1827 William Holloway. Lifted by William Richardson 10 Jan 1831.

1:283 - THIS INDENTURE - 20 Nov 1827 - Orlando Griffith, Lucy wife, James Clendenen, Sally wife formly Sally Griffith and Nancy Griffith heirs of William Griffith dec'd of Bath Co. to James Ross, Elizabeth wife formly Elizabeth Griffith, $70 paid for 40A land he now lives on, Cowpasture River...Orlando Griffith, James Clendenen, Nancy Griffith...witness - Fountain Morrison, Griffith Ross, John Shawer. Rec'd 11 Jun 1827 Oliver Callaghan.

THIS INDENTURE - 1 Mar 1827 - Rinehard Kimberline, Francis wife, to Jacob Kimberline, Henry Kimberline, $350 for 5 separate tracts, one 9th part of all five tracts in Rich Patch on the James River. First tract 680A granted to Michael Kimberline by patent 12 Aug 1794, neighbors - James Robinson, Patterson. Second tract, legally transfered from Samuel Porter to Michael Kimberline by deed 14 Apr 1795 rec'd in Botetourt Co. containing 48A. Third tract transfered from James Hanson and wife to Michael Kimberline deed dated 12 Dec 1809 rec'd in Botetourt Co. Containing 31A and 26 poles. Fourth tract indeeded by the same deed 90A and 93 poles. Fifth tract of 200A transfered to Michael by James Wright who held grant dated Sept 1785, Rinehard a full heir to the 9th part being his legacy left him by his father Michael Kimberline...Rinehard Kimberline, Francis Kimberline...release of dower by Stephen Hooks and Peter Pence. Rec'd Mar 1827 William G. Holloway.

1:286 - 9 Apr 1827 - Mounticue Allen debtor, William H. Terrill trustee, and John Allen Andrew Harmon creditors, all of Alleghany Co. Whereas John Allen and Andrew Harmon have become security of Mounticue Allen for payment of certain sums of money - 1 bond executed by Mounticue Allen, John Allen and Andrew Harmon 9 Apr 1827 for $42.04 payable to Alexander S. Hale. Other bond, 9 Apr 1927 for $120.75 payable to Robert Bratton.
Mounticue wanting to secure the sum's and release John and Andrew againist all which they may incur by becoming his security, in consideration of $1 paid by William Terrill for all his interest in the estate of George Wayt dec'd. which Mounticue accured by intermarrying with Kesiah Wayt of Alleghany Co. daughter of George dec'd, the estate consisting of negroes stock...Mounticue Allen, William H. Terrill, John Allen, Anthony (X) Harmon. Rec'd Apr 1827 William G. Holloway.

1:287 - THIS INDENTURE - 26 Jan 1827 - James Knox to Robert Skeen both of Alleghany Co., $85 for lot # 78 in Covington 1/4A...James Karns...Ack'd by John L. Boswell and Samuel B. Lowery. Rec'd Feb 1827 William Holloway.

1:288 - THIS INDENTURE - 20 Jan 1827 - Joseph Stillings, Jane wife to James Karnes Jr. both of Alleghany Co., $220 for lot # 81 in Covington on Third St. 1/4A, conveyed to Stillings by Thomas

Byrd...Joseph Stillings, Jane Stillings...release of dower by John Callaghan, and John Persinger. Rec'd Mar 1827 William Holloway.

1:290 - THIS INDENTURE - 8 Nov 1827 - Hazel Williams, Nancy wife of Greenbrier Co. to William Kyle of Alleghany Co., $230 for lots # 65 & 66 in Covington, 1/4A each...Hazel Williams, Nancy Williams...release of dower in Greenbrier Co. by Addison Frazer and Francis Ludington. Rec'd Dec 1827 Oliver Callaghan.

1:291 - 1 Jan 1828 - Francis Crutchfield of Alleghany Co. to Alexander Parris of Augusta Co., whereas Archibald Morris, Elizabeth wife in order to secure and provide payment of $1,979.97 due to George Sively by bond 17 Nov 1818 payable 1 Mar 1819 by indenture dating 6 May 1820 and admitted to recover in Bath Co. 13 Jun 1820 did convey to Francis Crutchfield and Moses H. Mann a tract in Allleghany Co. on Jackson River, where Richard Morris Sr. dec'd lived. Land consists of 117A, part of 2 tracts, 93A and 270A, 117A in possession of Edmund P. Walton. Land is known as Mom's Old Place. Sale to take place at Robert Skeen's Tavern in Covington. Sale subject to a decree of Superior Court of Chancery for Greenbrier Co. Nov term. Benjamin Morris plaintiff and Archibald Morris defendent, decree for $425.27, 115A sold by Benjamin to Archibald to be sold by marshall at sale. THIS INDENTURE - Francis Crutchfield to Alexander Parris 117A for $1,800...Francis Crutchfield...Ack'd 2 Jan 1828 William G. Holloway, rec'd Jan 1828 Oliver Callaghan. Lifted by Alexander Parris, no date.

1:295 - THIS INDENTURE - 8 Mar 1827 - Benjamin Haynes to William Snead, for $27 103A of Dunlaps Creek, upper end of land was conveyed to Benjamin Haynes by a deed from William Smith 28 Sept 1821 recorded in Monroe Co. 16 Oct 1821 containing 53A...Benjamin Haynes...witness - Joseph Damron, Cornelius Vanstavern, Samuel Kean. Rec'd Jun 1827 Oliver Callaghan. Lifted by Joseph Damron 25 Nov 1830.

1:296 - THIS INDENTURE - 13 Oct 1827 - John Taylor, Sally wife to Hugh P. Taylor, all of Alleghany Co., $530 for lot # 120 in Covington 1/4A. Same lot that was deeded by James Merry to Henry Dressler 16 Nov 1824, by Dressler and wife to John Taylor 8 Jan 1825...John

Taylor, Sally Taylor...release of dower by Samuel B. Lowery and John L. Boswell. Rec'd Nov 1827 Oliver Callaghan.

1:297 - THIS INDENTURE - 4 Dec 1827 - Hugh P. Taylor, Mary Ann C. wife to John Taylor, $470 for lot # 120 in Covington 1/4A. Lot conveyed to Hugh P. Taylor by John Taylor and wife 13 Oct 1827...Hugh P. Taylor, Mary Ann C. Taylor...release of dower by Samuel B. Lowery, and John Boswell. Rec'd 12 Dec 1827 Oliver Callaghan.

1:299 - THIS INDENTURE - 19 Jan 1828 - Susannah Clear to Conrad Lemon, both of Alleghany Co., $180 for 180A on west side of Cowpasture River. It first being granted to Susannah's father Jacob Clear 26 ? 1796, then to her by will recorded Botetourt Co...Susannah (X) Clear...Ack'd by Joseph D. Keyser and William H. Haynes. Rec'd Jan 1828 Oliver Callaghan.

1:300 - THIS INDENTURE - 1 Jan 1828 - James Merry, Mary wife of Alleghany Co. to Elisha Williams of Greenbrier Co., $101 for lot # 34 in Covington on Main St. Purchased at public sale in 1818...James Merry, Mary Merry...release of dower by Samuel B. Lowery and John Boswell. Rec'd Jan 1828 Oliver Callaghan.

1:302 - THIS INDENTURE - 18 Dec 1827 - Sarah Mann to John Shumate, $100 for 160A land joining Watkins and Willam Taylor dec'd. Sarah sells her dower right...Sarah Mann...Ack'd by John Callaghan and Charles Callaghan. Rec'd Jan 1828 Oliver Callaghan.

1:304 - 21 Jan 1828 - Amanda Taylor first part, William H. Terrill second part, John Shumate, Peter Smith third part, all of Alleghany Co. Amanda appointed administrator with will annexed of William Taylor dec'd. John and Peter are securties, and she wanting to indemnify them against any damages which they may sustain due to his defaults. William Terrill paid $1 for all land on which William Taylor lived at time of his death which he devised to Amanda...Amanda Taylor, William H. Terrill, Peter Smith, John Shumate...Rec'd Jan 1828 Oliver Callaghan.

1:306 - THIS INDENTURE - 1 Dec 1827 Matilda C. Carson of Cumberland Co. VA to Peter Pence of Alleghany Co., $220 for 100A agreeable to Treasury warrant granted to George Carson dec'd recorded in Botetourt from patent 1797. Located on Castels Run...Matilda C. Carson...Ack'd in Cumberland Co. by Tschar Woodson. Rec'd Jan 1828 Oliver Callaghan.

1:308 - 21 Jan 1828 - James Karnes debtor to William H. Terrill trustee. James indebted to John L. Boswell creditor for $345.97 due by bond 14 Jan 1828 payable to William Kyle and William Scott merchants, also to the firm Scott and Kyle $82.20 by bond 14 Jan 1828. William paid $1 for 2 lots # 80 & 81 in Covington with house...James Karnes, William Terrill. Rec'd Jan 1828 Oliver Callaghan.

1:309 - THIS INDENTURE - 24 Sept 1827 - William Burd, Mary wife of the town of Lynchburg to Isaac Steel of Alleghany Co., $115 for lot # 64 in Covington opposite of the store house of Scott & Kyle. This lot was conveyed to Burd by Hazel Williams...William Burd, Mary Burd...release of dower in the Corporation of Lynchburg by Abraham K. North and Albon McDaniel 29 Oct 1827. Rec'd Jan 1828 Oliver Callaghan. Lifted by I. Steel 12 Apr 1833.

1:311 - 2 Jul 1823 - William Fenwich of Henico Co. and Phillip Mayo of city of Richmond. On 21 Jun 1822, William intended to secure all and singular debts, so he executed a deed of trust to Samuel Clayton and others recorded in Henico Co. The following debts were not recollected and were omitted - Samuel Sublett $40, George Hutchinson $10, John Boyce $10, John Minchie $50, George Clark of KY $20.18, Lewis Webb $19, Augustine Davies $15, John Francis of Petersburg $60, William Cowan $8, Robert Gordon $59. William also being indebted to the President and Directors of banks of VA for $674, by 2 notes endorsed by Mathew Rice and Patrick Gibson. For the purpose of endimfing his endorsers he executed deed of trust to Charles J. Marmundo for 75A in Henrico by convance from Alice G. Williams executrise of William C. Williams and John G. Williams recorded 6 Sept 1819. Wanting to make further provisions for payment and at last term of general court judgement was rendered, on behalf of the commonwealth, against Mathew H. Rice, William Fehnwick, Allen Bernard, Mathew Houston, John Saunderson securities of said Rice for sum of $20,000 therefore

$5 paid to William Fenwick by Phillip Mayo for 19,254A of land in Botetourt Co. in 3 or 4 tracts conveyed to said William Fenwick, James Breckenridge and Mathew Harvey by deed recorded, William believes in general court. Lying near Becon Quarter Branch in Henrico Co near Richmond 3 A land conveyed to William by deed from Barlette Still recorded in general court Nov 1813, also 1A and 86 poles at Marison Hill in Henrico Co. conveyed to William by deed from Alexander Fulton and others recorded in court at Henrico Co. Mar 1818. Also 2, 1/2A lots in town of Manchester #'s 121 & 191 in plan of town conveyed to William by deed from Peyton Randolph. All right title interest claim property and estate in tract of land in Henrico Co. 15 1/4A on money or other proceeds which may arise from a sale there of after satisfying sum of money due David Bullack and to secure land conveyed in trust and in and to a tract of land in said Henirco Co. containing 75A being same mentioned before, should anything remain after satisfing the purpose of the deed of trust aforesaid, also all right title interest now existing on hereafter to decree by remainder or reversion in all and singular property real or personal conveyed to Samuel Clayton and others by deed of trust first mentioned. William may keep pocession of property. If sale of land does not satisfy debts then Phillip Mayo may sell books and personal property...William Fenwick...Ack'd in Henrico Co. by J. B. Whitlocke...Ack'd by Corporation of Richmond by William P. Thompson, and Preston Smith 2 Mar 1826. Rec'd Jan 1828 Oliver Callaghan.

1:316 - 1 Jan 1828 - Alexander Parris, Ellen wife of Augusta Co. debtor, William H. Terrill and Johathan Sively of Alleghany Co. trustees, George Sively creditor. Alexander indebted to George for $1,200 due by bond 1 Jan 1828. Paid $1 by William H. Terrill and Jonathan Sively for 3 tracts on Jackson River, known by Morris's old place. Boundaries may be ascertained by referance to deed by Francis Crutchfield to Alexander Parris by virtue of sale made by Francis under deed of trust by Archibald Morris and Elizabeth wife, to Francis and Moses Mann to secure money due by said Morris to George Sively, at which sale Alexander Parris became purchaser...Alexander Parris, William Terrill, Jonathan Sively, George Sively. Rec'd Jan 1828 Oliver Callaghan.

1:318 - 17 May 1827 - John A. Reed and William H. Terrill of Alleghany Co. are held and bound to the President and Directors of James River Company in the sum of $1,000. The condition of the bond is such that John has been appointed by David S. Garland, commissioner of the Kanawha Road and Navigation to be the reciever of tolls on the said gate to be situated at his own house, east of Alleghany Mt. He may deduct 9% for his pay...John Reed, William Terrill...Ack'd John Callaghan. Rec'd Jun 1827 Oliver Callaghan.

1:319 - 18 Jun 1827 - Johnson Reynolds of Greenbrier Co. first part, Joseph Damron administrator of William Herbert dec'd second part, Oliver Callaghan third part. William Herbert on 22 Jun 1825 to secure payment of $72 to Oliver did by indenture of trust convey to Johnson Reynolds 1 negro girl named Mariah. Joseph Damron, administrator, has paid Oliver. THIS INDENTURE - For $1 paid by Joseph Damron administrator of William Herbert dec'd to Johnson Reynolds with approbation of Oliver signed by his being party to these presents and Oliver has sold to Joseph Damron all estate right title and interest he and Johnson have in slave...Johnson Reynolds, Oliver Callaghan. Rec'd Aug 1827 William Holloway.

1:321 - 26 Jan 1827 - Joseph Barling trustee for city of Baltimore in Baltimore Co. MD and Charles Ridgely of Hampton of Baltimore. MD. Cause depending in Chancery Court of MD, Charles Ridgely was complainant and William McMechen and T. Heath were defendents. On 10 Jul 1826 it was decreed that property in case be sold and Joseph Barling be trustee to make sale. Joseph, on 13 Sept 1826, set up public sale in Baltimore of all title, claim and interest of William McMechen in 23,343A lying in Bath Co. and Botetourt Co. Charles Ridgely became purchaser for $1,000. THIS INDENTURE - Joseph Barling, trustee, for $1,000 sold to Charles Ridgely 23,343A in Bath Co. and Botetourt Co...Joseph Barling, trustee...witness - H. Bell, Fielder Israel...rec'd Balitmore by William Gibson. Rec'd 29 Sept 1827 Oliver Callaghan. Sent to John Jordan by George H. Payne 8 Apr 1836 per order.

1:323 - 13 Jan 1827 - Charles Ridgely of Hampton to John Jordan and John Irvine of Lexington, Rockbridge Co. by indenture 7 Apr 18? Made between John Hollowell, Rebecca wife of Philidelphia PA to Charles

Ridgely 2,800A in Rockbridge Co. on Handlys Mill Creek which land was orginally in Rockbridge Co. but by division were to be in Botetourt Co. and Bath Co. but now are in Alleghany Co. The first patent, 9 Jul 1787, to Jeremiah Warder, Jeremiah Parker, and Richard Parker who on 27 Dec 1809 granted to John Hollowell. THIS INDENTURE - Charles Ridgely to John Jordan and John Irvine for $1,000 land above mentioned...Charles Ridgely, Hampton...witness - Thomas Kelly, Henry B. Chent...Ack'd and rec'd in Baltimore MD by Joseph I. Ogden, Sam Pickering, and William Gibson...Certified by Charles W. Hanson. Rec'd 29 Sept 1827 Oliver Callaghan.

1:327 - 13 Jan 1827 - Charles Ridgely of Hampton Baltimore Co. MD first part, John Jordan and John Irvine of Lexington, Rockbridge Co. VA second part, Nicholas Brice of city of Baltimore surving trustee of Robert Long third part. Nicholas by indenture 26 Jan 1827 for all estate right title and interest of Robert Long patentee of tracts lying in Botetourt Co. One contains 6,997A, patented 27 Aug 1800 recorded Richmond book # 46 or 40 page 204. Another containing 50A, a third containing 1,100A , fourth containing 1,280A, fifth containing 8,703A mostly in Botetourt Co., but part in Bath Co. and Rockbridge Co. The last 4 tracts patented to Long 13 Aug 1805, recorded at the Land Office Richmond in bk # 54, pages 159, 161, 162, and 164. Also 2 tracts in Bath Co. patented 27 Aug 1800 for 3,000A recorded bk 46 page 215, second 2,210 & 1/2A, 12 Aug 1805 bk 54 page 160. THIS INDENTURE - Charles Ridgely to John Jordan and John Irvine for $10,000 all estate right and title of Charles Ridgely acquired and obtained by deed of conveyance from Nicholas Brice...Charles Ridgely, Hampton...witness - Thomas Kelly, and Henry B. Coherd...Ack'd and cert'd in Baltimore Co. by Joseph I. Ogden, Samuel Pickering, William Gibson, and Charles W. Hanson. Lifted by H. Jordan 22 Feb 1831.

1:330 - THIS INDENTURE - 17 Sept 1827 - John Jordon, Lucy wife, John Irvine, Selina Ann wife, to Edward Jordon and Samuel F. Jordon all of Rockbridge Co. paid $10 for all estate right title and interest to undivided half of 8 tracts of land purchased of Charles Ridgely (above previous deed)...John Jordon, Lucy Jordon, John Irvine, Selina Irvine...release of dower and ack'd in Rockbridge Co. by Robert White, and John McClelland 17 Sept 1827. Rec'd Oct 1827 Oliver Callaghan.

1:333 - 26 Jan 1827 - Nicholas Brice of Baltimore, surving trustee of Robert Long and Charles Ridgely of Hampton. Robert Long, 11 Aug 1807 executed deed of trust to Nicholas Brice and Josiah Pennington for 5 tracts lying in Botetourt Co. 6,997A & 50A & 1,100 & 1,283 1/2A & 8,703A. Nicholas and Josiah, trustees, sold land at public auction in Balitmore on 13 Mar 1809, Charles Ridgely purchased all 23,000A more or less for $9,000, 1/4 to be paid in 90 days, $74 in 180 days, $74 in 8 months, $74 in 12 months with interest. Charles paid first installment when due, to pay balance of whole purchase money of convenyance was made and executed by trustees to him, but before it was paid it was alledged by Charles Ridgely that said lands, including ore bank was covered by older patent belonging to John Hollowell Esq. of Philadelphia. It was agreed with the approbation of Sarah Long execuator of Robert that Charles Ridgely should purchase transfering part and then submitt to arbertration wheather money should be paid for interference deducted from balance. Charles did purchase for $4,600, 13 May 1810 from John Hollowell shortley after Josiah Pennington died, leaving Nicholas sole trustee. Charles submitted question of allowance to the award of William Lormon and David Winchester Esq. arbitrators 28 Jun last past, ruled Charles should be allowed out of purchase money leaving balance of $4,408.14. Charles did satisfy. Nicholus Brice wants another conveyance...THIS INDENTURE - Nicholus Brice to Charles Ridgely for $10 all title of Robert Long and of himself as surviving trustee to above tracts 7 in number patented to Robert...Nicholas Brice, surving trustee...witness - Samuel Myer, Jacob Mall...Ack'd, rec'd and cert'd in Baltimore 27 Jan 1827 by Jacob S. Mall, mayor, Samuel Rickering, Joseph Ogdan, William Gibson, and Charles W. Hanson. Rec'd Oct 1827 Olive Callaghan. Sent to John Jordan by George H. Payne 8 Apr 1836 per order.

1:338 - THIS INDENTURE - 24 Dec 1827 - Peter Pence, Elizabeth wife to Peter Helmintoller, both of Alleghany Co., $300 for land on Castels Run. Patented by George Carson, 15 Jun 1797, conveyed to peter by Matilda C. Carson, legal representative of Geoge Carson....Peter Pence, Elizabeth Pence. Rec'd Apr 1828 Oliver Callaghan.

1:339 - 19 Sept 1827 - Bond of $1,000 by Andrew Fudge, William A. Terrill, John Crow, George H. Payne, and George Sively to William B. Giles, Governor. Condition is as such that Andrew Fudge is appointed commissioner of Public Revenue for the year of 1828. Andrew Fudge, William H. Terrill, John Crow, George H. Payne, George Sively. Rec'd Oliver Callaghan.

1:340 - 23 Jul 1818 - Plat of Covington in Botetourt Co., on northeast side of Jackson River opposit the mouth of Dunlap Creek. Water St is 60 ft. broad and turns northeast. Bath St. is 50 ft. ? and ? Parallel to Water St. Walnut and Mulberry alleys are 15 ft. broad and run parallel to streets. First, Second, and Third streets are 50 ft. broad and cross other streets at right angles running northwest. All lots are 73 ft. 10 inches front and 147 ? back ? ? . More lots on southeast side. In all contains 38A and 115 poles...William Anderson, surveyor's office Botetourt Co.

1:341 - THIS INDENTURE - 7 Apr 1810 John Hollowell Esq., Rebecca wife of Philadelphia to Charles Ridgely of Hampton, $4,600 for 2,800A in Rockbridge Co. on Hanalys Mill Creek, patent 9 Jul 1787 to Jeremiah Wardes, Jeremiah Parker and Richard Parker who conveyed 26 Dec 1809 to John Hollowell...Neighbors - Michael Gores, James Simpson...John Hollowell, Rebecca Hollowell...witness - Mary Hollowell, Charlotte Capidy, William Parker...release of dower in PA by William Tilghman Esq. 7 Apr 1810...Edward D. Cafield and Henry Prabow justices for Philadelphia Co. Greetings - Rebecca unable to conveniently travel to court of VA we give you power to receive acknowledgment of conveyance aforesaid 20 Apr 1810 Peyton Drew...release of dower in Philadelephia 9 May 1810 by Edward D. Cafield, H. P. Prabow, John Barker, mayor...cert'd in PA by Peyton Drew. Rec'd Oct 1827 Oliver Callaghan.

1:347 - THIS INDENTURE - 28 May 1827 - William Griffith, Mary wife formely Mary Gully, John Gillaspie, Comfort wife formly Comfort Griffith, James Ross, Elizabeth wife formly Elizabeth Griffith, James Clendenen, Sally wife formly Sally Griffith, Nancy Griffith, Orlando Griffith, Lucy wife, all heirs of William Griffith dec'd of Bath Co. to Orlando Griffith of Bath Co., $300 paid for 130A on Cowpasture River...neighbor - James Ross...William Griffith, Mary

(X)Griffith...Rockcastle Co. KY release of dower by James Terrill 28 May 1827...certified by John Quinn. Rec'd 28 May 1827 Oliver Callaghan.

1:349 - 24 Jan 1828 - Reubin Knox debtor, Oliver Callaghan trustee, David Edgar creditor all of Alleghany Co. Reubin indebted to David in the amount of $60 due by bond ? Mar 1827, also the sum of ?. Oliver paid $1 for misc. household items and farm animals...Reubin Knox, Oliver Callaghan, David Edgar...witness - Fittius Turner, William Scott. Rec'd Feb 1828 Oliver Callaghan.

1:351 - 7 Jan 1828 - Oliver Callaghan, Elvira W. wife, to John Callaghan. Paid $1 for all title and interest in estate of Dennis Callaghan father being one undivided 10th part of 717A on Uglies Creek. Granted to Dennis 16 Jan 1801 forming in Bath Co. Tract is subject to Margaret Callaghan's third, she being the widow...Oliver Callaghan, Elvira W. Callaghan...release of dower by Samuel B. Lowery and Isaac Steel 7 Feb 1825. Rec'd Feb 1825 Oliver Callaghan.

1:352 - THIS INDENTURE - 7 Mar 1827 - Benjamin Haynes to Corneluis Vanstavern, both of Alleghany Co., $400 for 43A on Dunlaps Creek joining John Hardy. Conveyed to Benjamin by William Smith and recorded in Monroe Co...neighbor - William Snead...Benjamin Haynes...witness - Joseph Damron, Samuel Kean Sr., Samuel Kean Jr. Rec'd Oct 1827 William Holloway.

1:354 - THIS INDENTURE - 26 Jan 1848 - Henry Dressler, Elizabeth wife to Isaac Steel both of Alleghany Co., $150 for 100A patented by Henry Dressler alias Henry Tressler, 29 Sept 1823...Neighbors - George Sively, Helmintoller and the late Peter Wright...Henry Dressler, Elizabeth Dressler...release of dower by Samuel B. Lowery and John L. Boswell 15 Mar 1828. Rec'd Mar 1828 Oliver Callaghan. Lifted by I. Steel 12 Apr 1833.

1:356 - THIS INDENTURE - 1 Feb 1828 - Elisha Williams, Margaret wife to William Cary both of Greenbrier Co., $120 paid for lot # 34 in Covington 1/4A...Elisha Williams, Margaret Williams...release of dower in Greenbrier Co. by Addison Frazer,and Francis Ludington. Rec'd Mar 1828 Oliver Callaghan. Lifted by William Cary 22 Apr 1828.

1:357 - THIS INDENTURE - 1 Mar 1828 - Orlando Griffith, Lucy wife of Bath Co. to George Armentrout of Alleghany Co., $625 for 130A on Cowpasture River...neighbor - James Ross...Orlando Griffith, Lucy Griffith...witness - Joseph D. Keyser, William H. Haynes...release of dower by Joseph D. Keyser and William H. Haynes. Rec'd Mar 1828 Oliver Callaghan.

1:359 - THIS INDENTURE - 14 Apr 1827 - Samuel Brown, Francis wife to George Sawyer both of Alleghany Co., $40 for 17A on Dunlaps Creek, part of a tract of 110A granted Brown 26 Aug 1806...Samuel Brown, Francis Brown...release of dower by Sampson Sawyer and Joseph Damron. Rec'd May 1827 Oliver Callaghan.

1:360 - THIS INDENTURE - 12 May 1825 - Abraham Sybert to James P. Ragland. For clearing land and the fencing of 30A, all land lying between the branch running from Jones land down to the big house at the ? Spring and first hill in front of Abraham's house. This is good for 20 yrs, 15 May 1825 to 15 May 1845...Abraham Sybert, James Ragland...witness - Oliver L. Jones, John (X) Lewis. Rec'd Mar 1828 Oliver Callaghan.

1:361 - 10 Mar 1828 - Fleming Keyser, Nancy wife to Alexander Parris, both of Alleghany Co. Richard Morris late of Jackson River died intestate leaving 10 kids intitled to equial partition, among whom was a daughter, Francis who afterwards married Archibald Armstrong, who died leaving husband and kids to wit: Nancy wife of Fleming Keyser, George Washington Morris and John Armstrong, her heirs intitled to one 10th which belonged to their mother. The land was partition under a decree of Chancery Court of Staunton upon which 271A was assigned to Archibald Morris, son of Richard Morris and brother to Francis Armstrong, as embracing shares in real estate Archibald claimed and as a purchaser from his brother Benjamin Morris and from Archibald Armstrong, husband of Francis. Francis died before conveying her title. Archibald Morris under contract with Archibald Armstrong filed a bill in Chancery Court against Nancy, wife of Fleming Keyser and the other children and heirs of Francis to obtain a title of the one 10th share of Francis. When Nancy married Fleming he became a party to the suit, he filed his answer contesting in right of his wife the claim of Archibald Morris. The cause was heard at

Staunton Nov 1827. The court decreed that the one 10th belongs to Francis's children and heirs. Fleming and Nancy are willing to settle. THIS INDENTURE - Fleming Keyser, Nancy wife to Alexander Parris for $316 & 2/3 for all their interest in the real estate of Richard Morris...Fleming Keyser, Nancy Keyser...Teste - Jessie Davis...release of dower by William McClintic and Robert Bratton in Bath Co. Rec'd Mar 1828 Oliver Callaghan.

1:364 - THIS INDENTURE - 20 Nov 1827 - Rosannah Moyer to George Moyer, both of Alleghany Co., $50 paid for one full and undivided 9th of forgoing tracts which George Moyer Sr. dec'd left. First 60A granted to William Hunter, 1 Sept 1781 then conveyed to David Tate, by David and Comfort wife to George Moyer Sr., rec'd in Botetourt Co Oct 1790. Second 74A granted to George 1 Jul 1817, 130A all together...Rosannah (X) Moyer. Rec'd Dec 1827 Oliver Callaghan.

1:365 - 25 Nov 1826 - Surveyed for Elizabeth Kean, widow of David Kean, by the directions of Phillip Rogers, John Crow, Michael Erskine and James P. Ragland, commissioners appointed by court Oct term 1826. Her right of dower in the Tanyard place contains 82A...Joseph Damron. Rec'd Jan 1827 Oliver Callaghan.

1:366 - THIS INDENTURE - 25 Apr 1828 - John A. Holly, Elon wife of Greenbrier Co. to John A. Reid of Alleghany Co., $10 paid for 150A on Oglies Creek...John A. Holly, Elon Holly...Release of dower by David Hanna and Thomas Kirkpatrick in Greenbrier Co. 29 Apr 1828. Rec'd Jun 1828 Oliver Callaghan. Lifted by John Reid 19 Oct 1830.

1:367 - 22 Jun 1827 - Superior Court of Chancery - City of Richmond - Lewis Ensiminger Plaintiff against James Swann, Jean Sigismond Ehsenneh, Count of Redern, Henry LeMercier, Francis Walderman, Charles William Juste Jerome, Lewis Phillibert Brun Aufrynose, Charles Frederick Albert Schott, Jean Mathias Greeting, Francis Joseph Perot, David Cooper Swann, James Heath, auditor public accounts VA, and John Robertson Esq. Attorney General of VA, defendants. Consent of plaintiff and defendants, John Robertson and James E. Heath to proceed against other defendants who are out of the country. Appearing on a deed from defendant James Swan, plaintiff is entitled to 4 undivided 48th or 1/20 of lands mentioned of which 43 undivided 48th are conveyed and plaintiff is interested in the 20 undivided 48th by same deed conveyed for the benifit of the Count of Redern and others, his interest in 22/48, not appearing at this time, the court adjudged ordered and decreed that Col John Armistead, Henry Anderson, William H. Shields, Branch T. Archer, Charles Abraham and John Carter appointed commissoners for the purpose of partition of the lands in the bill mentioned, so as to set apart to plaintiff one 12th equal part...William W. Hening...In pursuance of order of Superior Court of Chancery - City of Richmond Jun 1827 in suit of Lewis Ensiminger, plaintiff and James Swan and other defendants. We, the 4 commissioners named in order have preceeded to partition off lands, except 5,000A in Harrison Co. that seem to have been excluded from said deed of James Swann of 22 Nov 1819, so as to set apart one equal 12th - they are the following tracts - 50,000A on stoney Indian in Monroe Co. and Giles Co., surveyed for Andres Berrs 16 Jun 1795, grant 26 Jan 1796 and conveyed by Benjamin Parris and wife 17 Oct 1796 to James Swann. 25,000A in Randolph Co, both sides of middle fork Monongalia River, survey 27 Nov 1794, grant 20 Jun 1795 to Hugh McAlister who conveyed to Aaron Vancleve Jr. and Benjamin Stevens, from Aaron and wife with Benjamin to James Swann. 30,000A Bath Co. west side of Jackson River, surveyed 25 Apr 1795, grant 26 Nov 1795 to Robert Young who sold to James Swann. Four other tracts containing together 60,000A in Bath Co. - 16,000A east side of Cowpasture River survey 14 May 1785, 8,500A on Greenbrier River at forks of Knox Creek and Slate Fork, survey 10 May 1795, 17,5000A on Doughlets Cockrans and Beaver Lick Creek, survey 5 Jun 1785, 18,000A east side of Greenbrier survey 20 May 1795. The above 4 tracts are registered in the Land Office under Treasury Warrant #1295 and granted to James Swann. Also another tract of 24,000A in Bath Co. on west side of Jackson River, survey 28 Nov ? granted to James Swann 26 Aug 1795. Another for 22,788A in Russell Co. on Clinch and Sandy River, survey 4 Mar 17? grant to James Swann 9 Jun 1796. Four more tract which contain together 10,000A in Monongalia Co. granted to Henry Banks, 4,000A on Benjamin Creek survey 21 May 1785, 2,000A on Buffalo Creek survey 28 May 1785, 2,000A on the right hand fork of Buffalo Creek, survey 11 Oct 1784, 2,000A on the right fork of Buffalo Creek, survey 10 Oct 1784. The last 4 tracts mentioned are subject of a suit in Richmond

Chancery Count, James Swann plaintiff and Henry Banks and others defendents - decree made Sept 1811 ordering Banks to convey to Swann lands. The decree is on appeal affirmed by Court of applett Dec 1816. One other tract of 33,000A on Cripple Creek and Knob Fork of Elk Creek in Wythe and Grayson Co., survey 23 Jan 1795 grante to James Swann 27 Aug 1795. Another tract of 1,000A in Montgomery Co. at Salt Pond Mt., head of Little Stoney and Johns Creek, surveyed 23 Sept 1794 for William Price, grant to James Swann, 27 Aug 1795. Another tract of 21,000A in Kanawha Co. on Coles River, survey 11 Jan 1795 granted to Benjamin Grayson Orr 24 Dec 1795, with his wife he conveyed to John Dawson who conveyed to James Swann. Two more tracts of 3,425A in Kanawha Co., that is to say 2,130A and 1,295A granted to James Swann 18 May 1803. Two more tracts 1,659A in Kanawha Co., 1,130A and 529A granted James Swann 19 May 1803. The above several tract are judged by us to be one fair and equal 12th...John Armestead, Henry Anderson, William H. Sheilds, and Charles Abraham.

1:371 - 16 Feb 1828 - Superior Court of Chancery Richmond - Lewis Ensiminger plaintiff against James Swann, Jean Sigismond Ehsenneh, Count of Redern, Henry LeMercier, Francis Walderman, Charles William Juste Jerome, Lewis Phillibert Brun Aufrynose, Charles Fredrick Albert Schott, Jean Mathias Greeting, Francis Joseph Purot, David Cooper Swann, James E. Heath, auditor public accounts, John Robertson Esq., Attorney General VA defendants. Henry Anderson being appointed commissioner who in name of James Swann and in name of defentants David Cooper Swann, Charles William Jeste Jerome, Lewis Phillibert Brund Aufrynose, trustees in deed excuted by defendant James Swann and in name of Charles William Juste Jerome, Lewis Phillibert Brun Aufrynose and of other defendent convey to said plaintiff the lands mentioned and set apart to plaintiff in a proper deed except the said plaintiffs interest in the 22 undivided 48's by deed conveyed for benifit of Count of Redem and others to be held by James Swann, trustees. The court doth allow each commissioner $5 per day to be paid by plaintiff...Teste - William G. Pendleton, clerk.

1:372 - THIS INDENTURE - 15 Apr 1828 - James Swann late of Boston in MA, David Cooper Swann, Charles William Juste Jerome, Lewis Phillibert Brun Aufrynose, Jean Sigismond Ehsenneh, Count of

Redern, Henry LeMercier, Francis Walderman, Charles Fredrick Albert Schott, Jean Mathias Greeting and Francis Joseph Perot, by Henry Anderson acting commissoner, to Lewis Ensiminger, late counselor to his royal highness the duke of Lichtenberg and his intimate secretary at Munich in the Kingdom of Bavaria, but now a resident of VA. Conforming to decree, give to Lewis all lands mentioned in report of commissioners, John Armistead, Henry Anderson, William H. Shields, and Charles Abraham as allowed and set apart...Signatures of all of the above by Henry Anderson...cert'd in Richmond by William Corvling and James McKeldal Aldermen 20 Jun 1828. Rec'd Jul 1828 Oliver Callaghan.

1:374 - 17 Jan 1828 - Bond of William H. Terrill, Robert Skeen, Benjamin Douglas unto the President and Directors of the Literary Fund in the amount of $2,000. Condition is as such that William H. Terrill has been appointed Treasure for the School Commissioners for the year ending Nov 1828...William H. Terrill, Robert Skeen, Benjamin Douglas...Teste Oliver Callaghan.

1:375 - 16 Jun 1828 - Bond of Oliver Callaghan and John Callaghan to John Holloway, Stephen Hooks, Jessie Davis, Isaac Steel, Charles Callaghan, and John H. Boswell, justices in the amount of $705.60. Condition is as such that Oliver has been appointed commissioner to receive from the sheriff the full amount of the county levy for 1828...Oliver Callaghan, John Callaghan...Teste Oliver Callaghan

1:375 - THIS INDENTURE - 26 Apr 1828 - John A. Holly, Elon wife of Greenbrier Co. to John A. Reid of Alleghany Co., $10 for 100A on Oglies Creek...John A. Holly, Elon Holly...release of dower in Greenbrier Co. by Thomas Kirkpatrick, and David Hanna 29 Apr 1828. Rec'd Jun 1828 Oliver Callaghan.

THIS INDENTURE - 22 Apr 1828 - Palser Helmintoller of Smith Co. TN to John Persinger of Alleghany Co., $500 for 200A on Potts Creek...Palser (X) Helmintoller. Rec'd 3 May 1828 Oliver Callaghan.

1:377 - THIS INDENTURE - 22 Apr 1828 - Palser Helmintoller of Smith Co. TN to John Persinger of Alleghany Co., $10 for 50A on Potts Creek...Palser (X) Helmintoller. Rec'd May 1828 Oliver Callaghan.

1:378 - THIS INDENTURE - 22 Apr 1828 - Palser Helmintoller of
Smith Co. TN to John Persinger of Alleghany Co., 410 for 50A of Potts
Creek...Palser (X) Helmintoller. Rec'd May 1828 Oliver Callaghan.

1:378 - 9 Jun 1828 - John Bradley to Mathew Sawyer both of
Alleghany Co., $275 for 1 stud horse, medicines, all Bosces bottles,
vials, trunk, saddle and bridle...John Bradley...teste - Joseph Damron,
Archer Sawyer. Rec'd 1828 Oliver Callaghan.

1:379 - 28 Oct 1826 - William McCallister, debtor, William Terrill,
trustee, James Merry, creditor, all of Alleghany Co. William indebted
to James for $66.86 due by writing obligatory under seal executed by
William to Richard Smith on 20 Mar 1828. He has a credit of $12.10
paid Dec 1821 and $2.00 paid 2 Jan 1822. The rights to the writing
obligatory is in James Merry as a partner of the firm of Richard Smith.
William in order to secure unto James the several debts executed to
William Terrill a deed for sundry property, 22 Mar 1825. Doubt has
arisen as the sufficiency of the property conveyed, James is willing
and desirous to secure this indenture of premises, $1 is paid by Terrill
for 3 calves, 1 colt...William (X) McCallister, William Terrill, James
Merry. Rec'd Apr 1828 Oliver Callaghan.

1:381 - THIS INDENTURE - 23 Jul 1828 - Elisha Knox Sr. for love
and affection for my daughter Margaret Parker, widow of Hugh Parker
dec'd, of Alleghany Co., $1 paid for 50A including 16A formerly
granted to John Dickerson patent 13 Aug 1763, formerly property of
John Robinson, assignee of Jacob Solom, located on Dunlaps
Creek...Elisha (X) Knox Sr. Rec'd 23 Jul 1828 Oliver Callaghan.

1:382 - THIS INDENTURE - 23 Jul 1828 - Elisha Knox Sr. for love
and affection for my daughter Susan Knox, widow of William Knox
dec'd of Alleghany Co. $1 paid for 170A survey 27 May 1789 on
Dunlaps Creek...neighbors - George Moyer dec'd, Kerr dec'd, formely
Uriah Humphries and David S...Elisha Knox Sr. Rec'd 23 Jul 1828
Oliver Callaghan.
Lifted by Joseph Damron 14 Nov 1833.

1:383 - 18 Aug 1828 - Hamilton Mann, Lewis T. Mann, Lewis on behalf
of himself, Archibald Mann, John M. D. Mann and Sarah Mann to John

Richardson. In pursuance of a decree of Superior Court of Chancery in Greenbrier Co. on 6 Jun 1826 $1 paid for land subject to the interfuse of George Sively's claim agreeably to a copy of the courses of a patent to Mary Mann dec'd for 55A...Lewis Mann, Hamilton Mann. Rec'd Aug 1828 Oliver Callaghan.

1:384 - THIS INDENTURE - 31 Mar 1828 - Hugh Cummings, Catherine wife to Michael Arritt both of Alleghany Co., $93 for one 4th part of 90A of land formly belonging to Hugh Cummings dec'd. Land located on Potts Creek...Hugh Cummings, Catherine (X) Cummings...witness - John Arritt, Henry Meyer, Absalom Cummings...release of dower by John Persinger, and John Arritt 15 aug 1828. Rec'd Aug 1828 Oliver Callaghan.

1:385 - THIS INDENTURE - 26 Aug 1828 -William A. Herford, acting sheriff for Michael Knootz, sheriff of Mason Co. VA to which administration of all and singular goods, chattles and credity as are not contained in last will and testament of John Johnson dec'd, with the will annexed, committed to the above sheriff, one part. Thomas David, second part, paid $1 for 560A on Wooly's Run, a branch of Jackson River. This is part of 1,000A granted to John 30 Sept 1796...neighbor - Pitzer...William A. Herford, for Michael Knootz sheriff of Mason Co. Rec'd Sept 1828 Oliver Callaghan.

1:387 - 10 Jun 1828 - Mounticue Allen, Kesiah wife, debtor, William Terrill, trustee, Henry Smith, creditor. Mounticue and Mary Wayt indebted to Henry Smith in the sum of $286.67 bond dated 10 Jun 1828. To secure the sum Mounticue paid $1 by William Terrill for the right and title to the estate both real and personal of George Wayt dec'd...Mounticue Allen, Kesiah L. Allen, Henry Smith, William Terrill...witness - George Susber, Benjamin Douglas, Peter Pence...release of dower by Joseph D. Keyser and Peter Pence, 10 Jun 1828. Rec'd 20 Jun 1828 Oliver Callaghan.

1:388 - 20 Sept 1828 - Thomas Newell, debtor, to John T. Anderson, trustee. Thomas indebted to John Gillaspie for $500 by bond to John A. Kerly, also to John I. Moosman for $1,173. To secure the sums $1 paid by John Anderson for 500A on Jackson River, part of 1,000A tract granted by patent to Simon Gillaspie 23 Oct 1804. Simon dec'd leaving 4 children, Simon, John, Rebecca Wilson, and Nancy Newell, wife of Thomas. Both daughters became entitled by descent. Thomas purchased Simons and Johns share, Rebecca still owns one 4th, although she is indebted to Newell to secure payment of which he holds her share...neighbors - Jacob Shaver, now owned by Griffith, Boston Hance...Thomas Newell, John T. Anderson. Rec'd 22 Sept 1828 Oliver Callaghan.

1:390 - 18 Aug 1828 - Moses H. Mann plaintiff vs William Mann defendant - in Chancery - report of Archibald M. Kincaid sheriff for Robert Kincaid, late sheriff, in obedience to a decree of this court, it appearing plaintiff recovered of defendant William Mann money with interest. THIS INDENTURE - 29 Aug 1828 - Archibald Kincaid to Joseph Damron both of Alleghany Co., $71 for lot # 44 on Water St. in Covington, 1/4A. Deed of conveyance with special warranty against the claim or claim of defendant William Mann and his heirs...Archibald M. Kincaid...ack'd 13 Sept 1828 Fittius Turner. Rec'd Sept 1828 Oliver Callaghan. Lifted by Joseph Damron Mar 1829.

1:392 - 5 Aug 1828 - Nathan Cox, of Alleghany Co., debtor, to John Steel of Rockbridge Co., trustee. Nathan to secure payment of $300 to Daniel Steel, creditor, as he is security for Nathan Cox to creditors and heirs of William Cox dec'd for $600 2 Jun 1827. John paid $1 for several farm animal, misc. household items, several books, and the current crop...Nathan Cox, John Steel...witness - Rachel Steel, Catherine Anderson. Rec'd Sept 1828 Oliver Callaghan.

1:393 - THIS INDENTURE - 26 Jan 1828 - John Rinhard, Rosanna wife to Michael Arritt, both of Alleghany Co., $600 for 3 tracts on Potts Creek, 107A part of 395A, first granted John Brown and William Brown, conveyed to Phillip Fisher by deed 15 Jun 1808, neighbor - Ester Rayhill. Second tract 50A granted to Phillip Fisher assignee of Henry Smith patent 2 Apr 1808, this tract is interlocked by part of 300A belonging to Michael Arritt. Third tarct contains 12 A granted to Phillip Fisher, patent 28 Oct 1807, neighbor - Brown...John Rinehard, Rosanna (X) Rinehard...release of dower by John Arritt and Joseph Damron. Rec'd Aug 1828 Oliver Callaghan.

1:395 - Bond of John Persinger, Andrew Fudge, Jacob Kimberline in the amount of $1,000 to William Giles, Governor. The condition is as such that Andrew Fudge has been appointed Commissioner of Public Revenue for the year of 1829...Andrew Fudge, Jacob Kimberline, John Persinger. Rec'd Oliver Callaghan.

8 Oct 1828 - William Patterson, Elizabeth wife, debtors, Oliver Callaghan, trustee, John Mallow and Jacob Kimberline, creditors. William and Elizabeth indebted to John Mallow in the amount of $87.48 bond dated this day and further sum of $80 bond dated 16 Apr 1828. They are also indebted to Jacob Kimberline in the amount of $90.75 due this date and the further sum of $68.50 bond executed, William to Jacob Kimberline, Henry Kimberline, administrators of Michael Kimberline dec'd, 7 Jul 1826. Last bond judgement obtained against William. Oliver paid $1 for ?05A in Rich Patch...neighbors - Joseph Grammars...William Patterson, no signature for Elizabeth, Oliver Callaghan, John Mallow, Jacob Kimberline...ack'd Stephen Hooks, George Mallow. Rec'd Oct 1828 Oliver Callaghan.

1:397 - THIS INDENTURE - 3 Oct 1828 - Isaac Gray, Lucy wife, Berkely Hardy all of Alleghany Co., to Jacob Kimberline, $136 paid for 190A in Rich Patch on Craigs Creek. Isaac and Lucy sell one 3rd and Berkely sells one 4th...Isaac Gray, Lucy (X) Gray, Berkely Hardy...release of dower by Stephen Hooks and George Mallow. Rec'd 9 Oct 1828 Oliver Callaghan.

1:398 - THIS INDENTURE - 31 Mar 1828 - Absalom Cummings, Rebecca wife to Michael Arritt, $93 for one 4th of a tract on Potts Creek, 90A, formally belonging to Hugh Cummings dec'd...neighbors - Kelly, and Brown...Absalom Cummings, Rebecca (X) Cummings...witness - John Arritt, Henry Meyer...release of dower by Isaac Steel and John Callaghan. Rec'd 21 Oct 1828 Oliver Callaghan.

1:400 - 13 Oct 1828 - Jessie Humphries debtor, Joseph Damron trustee, Hugh Duke, creditor, all of Alleghany Co. Jessie indebted to Hugh for $50, $1 paid by Joseph for 55A on Blue Spring Run. Land sold by Charles Callaghan to Jessie and William Humphries, William sold his share of 55A to Jessie, also part of a tract of 924A granted to

Jacob Persinger Sr....Jessie Humphries, Joseph Damron. Rec'd Oct 1828 Oliver Callaghan.

1:401 - THIS INDENTURE - 13 Apr 1828 - William F. Morton, Catherine wife to William Scott both of Alleghany Co., $45 paid for lot # 113 in Covington, 1/4A...William F. Morton, Catherine Morton. Rec'd Oct 1828 Oliver Callaghan.

1:402 - 21 Dec 1828 - Frederick Glassburn debtor, George Sively creditor, John Williams trustee all of Alleghany Co. Frederick indebted to George for $48.35 by bond 21 Dec 1828. John paid $1 for 2 tracts on Jacksons River. First tract 15A, 4th corner of David Glassburns survey of 110A, the 15A granted to Frederick 7 Jul 1827. Second tract 68A granted to Frederick 7 Jul 1827...neighbors Michael Mallow, David Glassburn...Frederick Glassburn, George Sively, John Williams...witness - Hugh P. Taylor. Rec'd Dec 1828 Oliver Callaghan. Lifted by George Sively 5 May 1829.

1:404 - 16 Dec 1828 - James Kibble debtor, Lewis Stuart of Greenbrier Co. trustee, Thomas Greigh of Greenbrier, creditor. James indebted to Thomas for $79.80 by bond 16 Dec 1828. Lewis paid $1 for farm animals and misc household items...James Kibble. Rec'd Dec 1828 Oliver Callaghan.

1:406 - 26 Nov 1828 - John Holloway debtor, Hugh P. Taylor trustee, William Scott and William Kyle merchants and co-partners in the firm of Scott and Kyle, all of Alleghany Co. John indebted to Scott and Kyle for $146 by bond 24 Nov 1828. Hugh paid $1 for 1 negro boy named Jack, 7 or 8 yrs old...John Holloway, Hugh P. Taylor, William Scott, William Kyle...ack'd by Fittieus Turner. Rec'd Dec 1828 Oliver Callaghan.

1:408 - 31 Dec 1824 - Francis Foster debtor, William H. Terrill trustee, Christopher Harmon creditor, all of Alleghany Co. Francis indebted to Christopher for $51.50 by single bill 18 Mar 1823. William paid $1 for farm animals...Francis Foster, William H. Terrill Christopher Harmon. Rec'd Nov 1828. Lifted by William H. Terrill 23 Sept 1829. Lifted by Terrill 23 Sept 1829.

1:409 - THIS INDENTURE -11 Dec 1828 - Hamilton Mann, son and devisor of Moses Mann dec'd, to John H. Peyton of Augusta Co. Moses in life had 2 grants on Falling Springs. First 250A, 28 Apr 1798 and the second 400A surveyed 11 May 1819, grant 1820. Moses will written in 1818 proved in Superior court, he devised land to his 4 surviving sons - Hamilton, Lewis, Archibald, and John. Hamilton sells his to Peyton for $250...neighbor - Henry Massie...Hamilton Mann...ack'd William S. Esthridge and William Young . Rec'd Dec 1828 Oliver Callaghan.

1:411 - 4 Nov 1828 - William H. Terrill and Robert Kelso executors of the will of James Merry dec'd trustee, Francis Crutchfield debtor, and George Sively creditor all of Alleghany Co. Francis on 18 Dec 1826 to secure payment of $134.38 to George Sively did by indenture of trust, 19 Dec 1826, convey to William and James 2 negro girls Patsy and Sally, 16 &15 yrs. Francis has paid debt. THIS INDENTURE - William and Robert to Francis, $1 paid for release of claim to slaves...William H. Terrill, Robert Kelso, executors of James Merry dec'd, Francis Crutchfield, George Sively. Rec'd Nov 1828 Oliver Callaghan.

1:413 - THIS INDENTURE - 24 Dec 1828 - Isaac Steel, Julia wife to Andrew M. Scott both of Alleghany Co., $1 paid for lot # 64 in Covington, 1/4A...Isaac Steel, Julia Steel...release of dower by Charles Callaghan and John Callaghan. Rec'd 24 Dec 1828 Oliver Callaghan.

1:414 - Robert Brooks Esq., Governor of VA - Greetings: Virtue of 5 land Treasury Warrants, #'s 6658, 14,678, 8478, 1,24?, 1566 granted to John Johnson 1,000A survey 15 Oct 1795 in Rich Patch...neighbors - John Crawford and William Wilson...Robert Brooke. Rec'd Aug 1828 Oliver Callaghan.

1:415 - THIS INDENTURE - 20 Jan 1829 - Samuel Merry, legal heir of James Merry dec'd, Mary Merry other heir, Robert Kelso executor for Mary, to John Shirkey, $1 for lots # 71 & 72 in Covington...Samauel Merry, Robert Kelso. Rec'd 20 Jan 1829 Oliver Callaghan.

20 Jan 1829 - Samuel Merry executor of James Merry, Robert Kelso, executor of Mary Merry to James Karnes, $1 for 3 lots # 106, 107, &

112 in Covington. The same lots purchased by Karnes of James 24 Aug 1818, Karnes had not received deed...Samuel Merry executor of James, Robert Kelso executor of Mary. Rec'd 20 Jan 1829 Oliver Callaghan.

1:416 - THIS INDENTURE - 20 Jul 1829 - Samuel Merry, legal heir of James Merry, Robert Kelso, executor of Mary R.Merry to Joseph Pinnell, Moses Persinger, Henry Dressler, Elisha Knox Jr., Charles Callaghan, Anthony Brunnemer, Charles Tolbert, all trustees of Episcopal Methodist Church, $1 for lot # 117 in Covington 1/4A...Samuel Merry, Robert Kelso. Rec'd 20 Jan 1829 Oliver Callaghan.

14 Jan 1829 - Articles of agreement between Samuel McCallister and Joseph Damron, $1,000 paid for 221A on Dunlaps Creek, survey 5 Aug 1826. Samuel will make title in fee simple 25 Dec 1833, Samuel has possession until then, and Joseph will retain several debts of Samuel until then, debts will be settled out of $1,000 including debt to Jane Pitzer. Joseph will furnish to Samuel and his brother James $250 to pay John Crain, due from the estate of John McCallister dec'd...neighbors - John Crain, James McCallister..Samuel (X)McCallister, Joseph Damron. Rec'd 19 Jan 1829 Oliver Callaghan. Lifted by Joseph Damron 9 Feb 1830.

1:418 - THIS INDENTURE - 24 Feb 1819 - James Merry, Mary R.wife, Samuel Merry of Botetourt Co., to Moses Mann Sr., $1 for lot # 97 in Covington 1/4A...James Merry, Samuel Merry, no signature for Mary...witness - Richard Smith, D. Callaghan, Benjamin T. Douglas...release of dower by Peter Wright and Joseph D. Keyser in Botetourt Co. Rec'd Jan 1829 Oliver Callaghan.

1:419 - THIS INDENTURE - 30 Sept 1828 - William Rice, Anna wife of Monroe Co. To George Meyers of Alleghany Co., $75 for undivided 9th of 2 tracts on Dunlaps Creek. First tract of 60A granted to William Hunter patent 1 Sept 1781, then conveyed to David Tate and Comfort wife, they to George Meyers, who is now dec'd, in Oct 1790 rec'd Botetourt Co. Second tract for 74A granted to George Meyers 1 Jul 1818, decended to Anna wife of William and to 8 other heirs...neighbor - Elisha Knox Sr....William Rice, Anna Rice...release of dower in Monroe Co. by James Handley and Henry Alexander 30 Sept 1828. Rec'd 13 Feb 1829 Oliver Callaghan.

1:420 - THIS INDENTURE - 10 Feb 1829 - Duiguid Pitzer, Sally wife to George Meyers, $75 for undivided 9th, part of George Meyers Sr. dec'd land on Dunlaps Creek. Two tract, one 60A and one 74A...Duiguid Pitzer, Sarah Pitzer. Rec'd 14 Feb 1829 Oliver Callaghan.

1:422 - THIS INDENTURE - 24 Jan 1879 - Duiguid Pitzer, Sally wife to Joseph K. Pitzer, $400 for all claim in one undivided 13th of the estate of Bernard Pitzer dec'd, except ½ to Jane Pitzer, widow. One tract in the mouth of Dunlaps Creek 1.?A, Bernard Pitzer lived on when died. Second 189A joining lands of James Merry 's estate near Covington. Third tract 124A joining lands of Thomas Mc? Sr., 54A joining John Sprowl's estate, 100A neighbor Francis Foster, 164A, 22A, 28A, 140A, 750A, 840A granted 10 May 1827 to the heirs of Bernard Pitzer. Also 420A in Botetourt Co., neighbor Peter Dagger dec'd, patent 1 Dec 1809, any interest they may have in 1.5A of land belonging to the heirs of John Sprowl dec'd which is in Chancery Court in Greenbrier Co...Duiguid Pitzer, Sarah Pitzer...release of dower by Samuel B. Lowery and Peter Pence 24 Feb 1829. Rec'd 24 Jan 1829 Oliver Callaghan. Lifted by Joseph K. Pitzer 21 Mar 1831.

1:424 - 30 Jan 1827 - Christopher Harmon bought on 24 Aug 1818 lot # 73 & 74 in Covington from James and Samuel Merry. It was not recorded, and Harmon sold to Isaac Steel. THIS INDENTURE - Samue Merry, heir of James Merry dec'd, Robert Kelso, executor of Mary R. Merry dec'd, heir of James Merry to Isaac Steel, $1 paid for lots # 74 & 74 in Covington...Samuel Merry, Robert Kelso. Rec'd 2 Feb 1829 Oliver Callaghan. Lifted by Isaac 12 Apr 1833.

THIS INDENTURE - 18 Jan 1829 - Samuel Merry, heir of James Merry, Robert Kelso, executor of Mary R. Merry, to Henry Dressler, $1 for lots # 35 & 36 in Covington 1/4A each...Samuel Merry, Robert Kelso. Rec'd 26 Jan 1829 Oliver Callaghan.

1:425 - THIS INDENTURE - 4 Jan 1829 - Samuel Merry, heir of James Merry, Robert Kelso executor of Mary R. Merry, to Joseph B.

Clark, $300 for lot #'s 17 & 18 in Covington 1/4A each...Samuel Merry, Robert Kelso...witness - William Scott, Joseph B. Stillings, James Hobbs. Rec'd 4 Feb 1829 Oliver Callaghan.

1:426 - THIS INDENTURE - 20 Feb 1819 - James Merry, Mary R. wife, Samuel Merry of Botetourt Co. to Alexander McClintic or Greenbrier Co., $1 for lot #'s 104 & 105 in Covington 1/4A each...James Merry, Samuel Merry, Mary R. Merry...witness - Richard Smith, D. Callaghan, B. T. Douglas...release of dower by Peter Wright and Joseph D. Keyser in Botetourt Co...James Merry executed deed for above lots, one to Robert McClintic and one to Moses McClintic...Alexander McClintic. Rec'd 22 Nov 1825 Oliver Callaghan.

1:427 - THIS INDENTURE - 22 Jan 1829 - Samuel Merry, heir of James Merry, Robert Kelso, executor of Mary R. Merry, to Charles Baldwin assignee of William Clark attorney for Babel Benson, heir of Andrien Benson, $49 for lot # 77 in Covington 1/4A...Samuel Merry, Robert Kelso. Rec'd 26 Jan 1829 Oliver Callaghan.

1:428 - THIS INDENTURE - 30 Jan 1828 - Samuel Merry, heir of James Merry, Robert Kelso executor of Mary R. Merry to James Sharky of Botetourt Co., $1 for lot # 96 in Covington 1/4A orginally sold by James Merry to James Sharky...Samuel Merry, Robert Kelso. Rec'd 2 Feb 1839 Oliver Callaghan.

1:429 - 14 Feb 1829 - Samuel Merry of St. Louis MO equal heir of James Merry appoint George H. Payne to be my attorney...Samuel Merry. Rec'd 14 Feb 1829 Oliver Callaghan.

2 Feb 1829 - Trust deed requires sale to be advertised in the newspaper. William Beverly, Samual Merry, Robert Kelso executor of James Merry, and the said Elisha Knox, trustee depose of advertising...William (X) Beverly, Samuel Merry, Robert Kelso, Elisha Knox. Rec'd 2 Feb 1829 Oliver Callaghan.

1:430 - THIS INDENTURE - 13 Feb 1829 - Samuel Merry, heir of James Merry, Robert Kelso executor, to William Kyle and William Scott, $350 for lots # 85, 86, 109, & 110 in Covington 1/4A each...Samuel Merry, Robert Kelso. Rec'd 13 Feb 1829 Oliver Callaghan.

2 Feb 1829 - John Cook owes $1,100.65 to James Merry estate. Executors Samuel Merry and Robert Kelso agree to further indulge until Dec next, no interest. Executor and Elisha Knox trustee agree advertising sale in papers shall be disposed of, instead advertise at court house...Samuel Merry, Robert Kelso, John Cook, Elisha Knox. Rec'd 2 Feb 1829 Oliver Callaghan.

THIS INDENTURE - 16 Feb 1829 - Samuel Merry heir of James Merry, Robert Kelso executor, to John Arritt, $1 for lot #2 in Covington 1/4A...Samuel Merry, Robert Kelso. Rec'd Feb 1829 Oliver Callaghan.

1:432 - 16 Feb 1829 - Samuel Matheny debtor, Douglas B. Layne trustee, Thomas Karnes creditor. Samuel indebted to Thomas for $41 by bond. Douglas paid $1 for farm animals and misc household items...Samuel Matheny, Douglas B. Layne, Thomas Karnes...testee - Henry Conner, C. Vanstavern, James Brown. Rec'd Feb 1829 Oliver Callaghan.

THIS INDENTURE - 17 Mar 1828 - Conrad Fudge, Elizabeth wife, to George Dressler, both of Alleghany Co., $10 for 1A located on Jackson River, joining Elizabeth Dressler's dower...Conrad Fudge, Elizabeth Fudge...release of dower by John Persinger, and George Mallow 17 Mar 1828. Rec'd Feb 1829 Oliver Callaghan.

1:434 - THIS INDENTURE - 7 Mar 1828 - Andrew M. Scott, Rachel wife to Isaac Steel, $1 for lot # 53 in Covington 1/4A...Andrew M. Scott, Rachel C. Scott. Rec'd 7 Mar 1829 Oliver Callaghan.

1:435 - 23 Oct 1824 - Michael Vincent of White Co. TN owns lots # 20, 21, 31, 32, 83, & 84 in Covington. I appoint John Vincent and John Hinchmon my attorneys to sell the aforesaid lots...Michael Vincent...State of TN White Co, acknowledged by Jacob A. Law and John H. Anderson Oct 1824. Rec'd 21 Feb 1829 Oliver Callaghan.

1:436 - THIS INDENTURE - 20 Apr 1829 - William H. Terrill, Elizabeth wife to William Scott and William Kyle, $550 for lot # 84 in Covington 1/4A...William H. Terrill, Elizabeth Terrill...ack'd Fittius Turner. Rec'd Apr 1829 Oliver Callaghan. Lifted by William Scott 20 Nov 1830.

1:437 - THIS INDENTURE - 27 Dec 1828 - Lewis L. Mann, Hamilton Mann, Archibald Mann, John Mann to Jane Gibson, Lyndia Gibson, Thomas M. Gibson. $500 for 200A on Indian Draft...neighbors - John Shumdle and Watkins heirs...Lewis L. Mann, Hamilton Mann, Archibald Mann, John Mann. Rec'd 1829 Oliver Callaghan.

1:438 - THIS INDENTURE - 16 Feb 1827 - Jacob Wolf, Mary Elizabeth wife to Abraham Wolf Jr., $50 for 36A on Potts Creek, land where Abraham now resides, being part of land on which Jacob resides which was conveyed from John Wolf, Magdalene wife on 18 Oct 1798, 108A recorded in Sweet Springs...Jacob Wolf...ack'd John Arritt and John Persinger 6 Nov 1828. Rec'd May 1829 Oliver Callaghan. Lifted by Abraham Wolf 16 May 1835.

1:440 - THIS INDENTURE - 13 Sept 1828 - Joshua Wood, Mary wife of Shenandoah Co. to Absalom Cummings of Alleghany Co., $1,000 for 135A on Indian draft. Joshua purchased from Benjamin Sweeney...Joshua Wood, Mary Wood...release of dower by Wharton Jones and Daniel Stover in Shenandoah Co. 13 Sept 1828. Rec'd Apr 1829 Oliver Callaghan. Lifted by A. Cummings 13 Apr 1830.

1:441 - THIS INDENTURE - 11 Apr 1829 - George Sively, Mary wife to Samuel Grose both of Alleghany Co., $500 for 265A on Cold Spring Run part of a 400A patent, 8 Aug 1799 part of which, 200A was sold to George 18 Sept 1820 by John McClintic, Moses McClintic, Sarah McClintic, Robert and Jane McClintic and Jane Mann...neighbor Archibald Mann...George Sively, Mary (X) Sively...release of dower by Samuel B. Lowrey and Isaac Steel 22 Apr 1829. Rec'd May 1829 Oliver Callaghan.

1:443 - 21 Apr 1829 - Samuel Grose, Nancy wife debtors, Jonathan Sively trustee, and George Sively creditior. Samuel indebted to George for $448., $1 paid by Jonathan for 265A on Cold Spring

Run...neighbor - Archibald Mann...Samuel Grose, Nancy Grose, George Sively...release of dower by Samuel B. Lowrey and Isaac Steel 22 Apr 1829...ack'd by Fittius Turner. Rec'd May 1829 Oliver Callaghan.

1:446 - THIS INDENTURE - 11 May 1829 - Charles Dew, Nancy wife to Michael Arritt, $24 for 18A on Potts Creek. Tract part of patent to Samuel Dew of 2,274A, 26 Jan 1799, decended to Charles as heir of Samuel...Charles Dew, Nancy Dew...witness - John Persinger, John Arritt...release of dower by John Persinger and John Arritt 11 May 1829. Rec'd Jun 1829 Oliver Callaghan. Delivered to Joseph Damron 2 Apr 1832.

1:448 - THIS INDENTURE - 12 Feb 1829 - John Damron of Washington Co. TN to Josesph Damron of Alleghany Co., $350 for 1 undivided 5th of 2 tracts on Dunlaps Creek. Both tracts are part of 185A granted Edward McMullin 3 Aug 1771. First tract conveyed by Joseph McMullin, Jane wife by deed 18 Dec 1805 (rec'd 19 May 1806 at Sweet Springs) to Joseph Damron 120A. The other tract of 39A conveyed by Valentine Jones, Loviah wife 16 Sept 1812 (rec'd Sept 1812 in Monroe Co.) to John Damron. This land has decended to John being one of the heirs of John Damron Sr....John Damron...witness - William Damron, James McCallister, Christopher Damron, Samuel McCallister, Andrew Damron. Rec'd Jun 1829 Oliver Callaghan. Lifted by Joseph Damron 9 Feb 1830.

1:450 - 15 Ju 1829 - John Callaghan, Sampson Sawyer first part, John Hardy second part. John Hardy, Elizabeth wife on 12 Apr 1823 to secure payment of $420 to John Reese did by indenture convey to John Callaghan and Sampson Sawyer land on Dunlaps Creek, 122A, 10 poles. The land was conveyed to John Hardy Apr 1823 from John Reese, 66A, 19 poles of the 122A, 10 poles it being the lower eastwardly end of old tract to Samuel Pogue Sr. by patent 13 Jul 1787, 50A of the 122A, 10 poles joins the old tract. Also 5A, 79 poles of the 122A, 10 poles is part of a survey of 21A that joins the old tract...neighbor - Smith. John Hardy has paid John Reese. John Reese had assigned 1 bond to Alexander Dunlap, 4 Oct 1826. THIS INDENTURE - John Callaghan, Sampson Sawyer to John Hardy for $1, with consent of John Reese confirm to John Hardy all rights to land above mentioned...John Callaghan, Sampson Sawyer. Rec'd Jul 1829 Oliver Callaghan.

1:452 - 29 Nov 1825 - Received from John Hardy $378.25, 3/4 cents in consequence of a deficiency in land I sold him on Dunlaps Creek which was estimated at 42 2/25A, 37 poles, at a rate of $8.85 per acre, and 2 mills. The rate per acre Hardy was to give me for land I sold him. The amount he paid is in full of a bond which I hold or did hold on John Hardy for $270. Bond given for part pay of land leaving a sum of $180.25 3/4 part of a bond executed to me for $150, which I assigned to Alexander Dunlap, leaving a balance due from Hardy of $42.74 1/4. I have also sold to John for $52 to be paid to Dunlap for total of $93.74 1/4 when paid. John Callaghan and Sampson Sawyer trustee of deed of trust 12 Apr 1823 will make release deed for land...John Reese...witness - Joseph Damron, George Sawyer. Rec'd Jul 1829 Oliver Callaghan. Received 4 Oct 1826 of John Hardy $93.74 1/4...Alexander Dunlap. Rec'd Jun 1829 Oliver Callaghan. Lifted by John Hardy Dec 1830.

1:453 - THIS INDENTURE - 16 Apr 1829 - Thomas Davis to Bennet Tinsley both of Alleghany Co., $1 paid for 114A of land on Jackson River. This land is part of land purchased from William A. Heaford administrator, with will annexed, of John Johnson...neighbor Rebecca Methaney...Thomas Davis. Rec'd Jul 1829 Oliver Callaghan.

1:455 - THIS INDENTURE - 30 Nov 1828 - Lucy Gray, executor of George Hardy dec'd, William Hardy to Henry Kimberline, $36 for one 4th of a tract on Craigs Creeks formly belonging to George Hardy...Lucy (X) Gray, William Hardy...ack'd Stephen Hooks and Jacob Kimberline 30 Oct 1828. Rec'd Jul 1829 Oliver Callaghan.

1:456 - 18 Jul 1829 - John Holloway debtor, William H. Terrill trustee, William Scott creditor. William Holloway and John Holloway indebted to William Scott in the amount of $82.44, by bond executed 25 Dec 1825, to Peter Pence administrator of Patrick Millhollin dec'd, 24 Apr 1829. Bond was assigned to William Scott 26 Jun 1829. THIS INDENTURE John Holloway to William H. Terrill, $1 for one negro boy name Jack...John Holloway, William H. Terrill. Rec'd 18 Jul 1829 Oliver Callaghan.

1:457 - 18 Jul 1829 - John Holloway debtor, George H. Payne trustee, George Sively creditor. John indebted to George in the amount of $100.81 by bond executed to Hazekiak Dodge on 15 Jul 1829. THIS INDENTURE - John Holloway to George H. Payne, $1 paid for 1 negro boy named Harrison...John Holloway, George H. Payne. Rec'd Jun 1829 Oliver Callaghan.

1:458 - THIS INDENTURE - 15 Jun 1829 - Thomas T. White to Hugh Duke both of Alleghany Co., $20 for the right and title of my fathers estate, will recorded in Bedford Co., after the death of my mother Lucy. Also White's right and title to the estate of Henry Latham dec'd, left by him to wife Polly S., alais Polly S. Aby recorded in Bedford Co...Thomas White. Rec'd Jul 1829 Oliver Callaghan.

1:459 - THIS INDENTURE - 15 Jun 1829 - Adam Persinger, attorney for Polly Faught wife of George Faught of Jackson Co. OH, Barbara Persinger wife of William Persinger of Green Co. OH, Margaret Persinger wife of Jacob Persinger of Green Co. OH, Rebecca Dudding wife of John Dudding of Kanawha Co. VA and George Persinger to Nathan Bush of Alleghany Co., $1 for all right and title and interest as heirs of Christopher Persinger to 11A on Blue Spring Run. Land is part of a tract of ?A sold to Christopher... signatures of all of the above by Adam Persinger. Rec'd Jun 1829 Oliver Callaghan.

1:460 - ? Jan 1829 - William Persinger, Barbary wife of Green Co. OH, son of Christopher Persinger and heir to one 11th of 11A on Blue Spring Run do appoint Adam Persinger of Botetourt Co. our lawful attorney to sell land...Barbara Persinger...witness - Jacob Persinger, Warner Maddon...release of dower by Joseph Hamill in Green Co. OH 20 Jan 1829...acknowledged by Josiah Grover. Rec'd Jul 1829 Oliver Callaghan. Lifted by Adam Persinger on Apl 1835.

1:462 - 25 Mar 1828 - George Faught, Polly wife of Jackson Co. OH, she being legal heir and child of Christopher Persinger dec'd intestate, appoint Adam Persinger of Botetourt Co as our attorney to sell my share of 1A out of 11A...George (X) Faught, Polly (X) Faught...acknowledged and rec'd in Jackson Co. OH by John B. Gilliland and A. M. Faulkner 25 Mar 1829. Rec'd Jul 1829 Oliver Callaghan. Lifted by Adam Persinger on Apl 1835.

1:463 - 9 Apr 1829 - Jacob Persinger, Margaret wife of Green Co. OH, Jacob being heir of Christopher Persinger dec'd, appoint Adam Persinger as our attorney to sell 1A our share out of 11A located on Blue Spring Run...Jacob Persinger, Margaret (X) Persinger...witness - David Dunlap...release of dower by Josiah Grover and David Dunlap in Green Co. OH 9 Apr 1829. Rec'd Jul 1829 Oliver Callaghan. Lifted by Adam Persinger 1835 Apl.

1:464 - 29 Jan 1829 - John Dudding, Rebecca wife of Kanawha Co. VA, she being a child and heir of Christopher Persinger dec'd to appoint George Persinger as our attorney to sell my share of 1A out of 11A located on Blue Spring Run....John Dudding, Rebecca (X) Dudding...ack'd and release of dower in Kanawha Co. by James Staton, James B. Rust, and Alexander W. Quarrien 29 Jan 1829. Rec'd Jul 1829 Oliver Callaghan. Lifted by Adam Persinger 1835.

1:466 - THIS INDENTURE - 23 Aug 1819 - John Wright, Catherine wife, Moses Persinger, Charlotte wife, John Persinger, Rachael wife, John King, Isbella wife, George Karnes, Elizabeth wife, George Faught, Margaret (Polly) wife, Jacob Persinger, Margaret wife by their attorney Moses Persinger, as to Faught, Jacob Persinger, George Persinger, William Persinger, Barbara wife, Adam Persinger to Nathan Bush, $1 to each paid for 11A on Blue Spring Run including Powder Mill...signatures with X George Karnes, Elizabeth Karnes, Rachael, Isabella, William Persinger, all signed by attorney Moses Persinger, Adam Persinger, George Persinger...release of dowers for Rachael and Isabella in Botetourt Co. by John Moore, George Saffarran and John M. Bowyer 23 Aug 1819...release of dowers in Allaghany Co. for Charlotte by John Arritt and John Persinger. Rec'd 15 Jun 1829 Oliver Callaghan.

1:468 - 13 Oct 1829 - George Washington Morris of Bedford Co. TN appoint Fleming Keyser as my attorney to receive all of which I am entitled as a child of Francis Armstrong, my mother, who was a child and heir of Richard Morris dec'd...George Washington Morris...acknowledged by Isaac Steel and Samuel B. Lowrey 15 Oct 1829. Rec'd Oct 1829 Oliver Callaghan. Lifted by G. W. Morris 15 Oct 1829.

1:469 - THIS INDENTURE - 10 May 1827 - Ephraim Simmons, Ruth wife to Jacob Wolf, $30 paid 20A on Blue Spring Run, part of a plantation Simmons now lives on...Ephriam Simmons, Ruth (X) Simmons...release of dower by John Arritt and Michael Arritt. Rec'd Sept 1829 Oliver Callaghan.

1:471 - 18 May 1829 - James Karnes debtor, William H. Terrill trustee, John L. Boswell creditor. James to secure payment for 2 bonds made by him, one to John Boswell for $345.97, Jan 1828, the other to Scott and Kyle for $82.20 4 Jan 1828 did by indenture 25 Jan 1828, rec'd Alleghany Co., 2 lots in Covington # 80 & 81. Lots sold for $300 to John L. Boswell...William Terrill. Rec'd Aug 1829 Oliver Callaghan.

1:472 - THIS INDENTURE - 28 Aug 1829 - Andrew McCallister to Robert Skeen both of Alleghany Co., one blk horse for undivided interest, 9th, of 3 tracts subject to dower of Barbara McCallister. First tract of 80A on Jackson River, patented to John McCallister 6 Jul 1812, second tract of 110A on the west side of Jackson River patented to John McCallister 22 May 1815. The third tract of 50A patented to Thomas McCallister 14 May 1803, conveyed from Thomas McCallister to John McCallister...neighbors - Thomas McCallister dec'd, Moses Mann, James Robinson heirs, Bernard Pitzer dec'd...Andrew McCallister. Rec'd 28 Aug 1829 Oliver Callaghan.

1:472 - THIS INDENTURE - 18 Sept 1829 - James Gilliland, Mary wife to David Bowyer both of Alleghany Co., $2 for 2 tracts on Potts Creek. First 189A John Wright sold to James Gilliland patented 25 Nov 1825, second tract of 19A patent 10 Aug 1827 to James...neighbors Johnstons...James Gilliland, Mary Gilliland...release of dower by John Persinger, and John Arritt. Rec'd Sept 1829 Oliver Callaghan.

1:476 - 23 Oct 1829 - George Armentrout, Catherine wife of Bowling Green Warren Co. KY appoint David Armentrout our attorney to receive as 1 of the legal heirs of William Smith dec'd...George Armentrout, Catherine Armentrout...certified in Alleghany Co. by Samuel B. Lowrey, and Isaac Steel. Rec'd Oct 1829 Oliver Callaghan. Lifted by David Armentrout 23 Oct 1829.

1:477 - 15 Aug 1829 - Thomas T. White debtor, Andrew Fudge trustee, Silas Latham and Hugh Duke creditors. Thomas indebted to Silas for $114.61 by bond, 1825 and to Hugh for $20 by bond 15 Aug 1829. Andrew paid $1 for Thomas's interest in a negro and the personal property left to Lucy White by her mother, widow of James White of Bedford Co....Thomas White, Andrew Fudge, Hugh Duke. Rec'd 15 Aug 1829 Oliver Callaghan. Lifted by Thomas White May 1830.

1:479 - THIS INDENTURE - 2 Sept 1829 - Henry Dressler, Elizabeth wife, Adam Quickle, Margaret wife, Joseph B. Clark, Christina wife of Allehgany Co. to Henry Pence of Monroe Co., $1700 for all rights in lots on Jackson River - Henry's lots, #1 9A of the old tract #27 of the same containing 2A 20 poles, also #2 of 200A containing 11 1/2A. Lot #2 contains as follows, lot # 11 of old tract 4A, # 17 same tract 1 1/2A, # 15 of 200A containing 10A as stated before considered second lot of Henrys as laid off. Lot # 3 contains lot #13 of old tract, 3?A and # 4 of 200A containing 10A being amont of lot # ?. Next lot # 4 containing lot # 15 of old tract 4A and #1 of tract of 200A containing 10A together with dower rights of Elizabeth Dressler at her decease as well as that of Moses Dressler dec'd, being one of the legatees of Henry Dressler dec'd whose part was one 16th part of land estate of Henry dec'd. Second that of Adam Quickle, Mary wife which intended to be sold as named unto Henry Pence and contain in lot # 14 of old tract of 400A, and lot # 5 of 200A tract containing 10A altogether with dower right of Elizabeth Dressler at her decease as well as Moses Dressler dec'd being 1 of legatees of Henry Dressler dec'd whose part is one 16th. Thirdly Joseph B. Clark, Christine wife to be sold to Henry Pence follows - lot # 2 containing 1A 30 poles and # 6 of tract of 200A containing 2A with dower rights same as above and rights to Moses Dressler dec'd same as above...Henry Dressler, Elizabeth (X) Dressler, Adam (X) Quickle, Mary (11) Quickle, Joseph B. Clark, Christine (V) Clark. Rec'd Sept 1829 Oliver Callaghan. Lifted by Quickle 1830.

1:481 - THIS INDENTURE - 2 Sept 1829 - Henry Dressler, Elizabeth wife, William Dressler, Margaret wife, George Dressler, Malinda wife, Jacob Dressler to Adam Quickle all of Alleghany Co., $1 for all right to land in Rich Patch on Blue Spring Run. Bequested to us by Henry Dressler dec'd...neighbors - Samuel Irwin, Jacob Wolf, George

Ester...Henry Dressler, Elizabeth (X) Dressler, William Dressler, Margaret Ann Dressler, George Dressler, Malinda Dressler, Jacob Dressler. Rec'd Sept 1829 Oliver Callaghan. Lifted by Adam Quickle 1830.

1:482 - THIS INDENTURE - 2 Sept 1829 - George Dressler, Malinda wife of Alleghany Co. to Henry Pence of Monroe Co., $350 for 3 lots. First lot George purchased of Conrad Fudge, Elizabeth wife, same as George now resides on, to the line of Elizabeth's Dressler's dower containing 1A. Second lot # 12 part of old tract of Henry Dressler dec'd containing 3 3/4A. Third tract # 3 of 200A containing 9 1\4A bequested by my father Henry Dressler. Also all right in dower of mother Elizabeth Dressler and interest in lot of Moses Dressler dec'd..neighbor - Fudge...George Dressler, Malinda Dressler. Rec'd 3 Sept 1829 Oliver Callaghan.

1:485 - THIS INDENTURE - 24 Sept 1829 - Elisha Knox, Agnes wife to Margaret Parker both of Alleghany Co., $1 for 16A on Dunlaps Creek where Margaret now resides...Elisha Knox, Agnes Knox. Rec'd 26 Sept 1829 Oliver Callaghan.

1:486 - THIS INDENTURE - 26 Sept 1828 - Elisha Knox, Agnes wife to Joseph Damron both of Alleghany Co., $700, to be here after paid and $300 paid now for 3 tracts on Dunlaps Creek. First tract of 59A part of 66A granted to Edward McMullin by patent 3 Aug 1771 in Augusta Co. Second tract of 150A granted to John Knox by patent 6 Aug 1810, third tract 40 1/2A, residue, part of 50A granted Elisha patent 29 Sept 1823, last two tract rec'd in Botetourt Co. In all 250A...Elisha Knox, Agnes Knox. Rec'd Oct 1829 Oliver Callaghan. Lifted by Joseph Damron 9 Feb 1830.

1:488 - THIS INDENTURE - 29 Sept 1829 - Henry Dressler, Elizabeth wife to Samuel Neville, $1,000 for 2 lots in Covington # 35 & 36, 1/4A each...Henry Dressler, Elizabeth (X) Dressler...release of dower by Isaac Steel and Samuel B. Lowrey...certified by Fittius Turner. Rec'd Oct 1829 Oliver Callaghan.

1:489 - THIS INDENTURE - 29 Sept 1829 - Henry Dressler, Elizabeth wife to Adam Dressler, $260 for all right to estate of Charles Dressler dec'd. Decended to Elizabeth upon the decease of her father Charles, except that part now held in dower rights...Henry Dressler, Elizabeth Dressler...release of dower by Samuel B. Lowrey and George Mallow, ack'd by Fittius Turner. Rec'd Oct 1829 Oliver Callaghan.

1:490 - 29 Sept 1829 - Samuel Neville, Maria wife debtors, Samuel B. Lowrey trustee, Henry Dressler creditor. Neville indebted to Henry by several bonds, $136.97 on 16 Jun 1828, also $136.97 16 Jun 1828, also $136.97 16 Jun 1828, also $136.97 16 Jun 1828, in all $547.88. Credit given to first bond of $18.60, $1 paid by Lowrey for 2 lots in Covington # 35 & 36, 1/4A each...Samuel Neville, Maria Neville, Samuel B. Lowrey...release of dower by John P. Boswell and George Mallow. Rec'd 29 Sept 1829 FittiusTurner for Oliver Callaghan.

1:493 - 24 Jul 1829 - Lewis Ensiminger of Monroe Co. appoint Joseph Damron power of attorney to sell all land in Bath and Alleghany Co. First tract 30,000A, second 24,000A, land conveyed to Lewis by Henry Anderson commissioner order of Superior Court of Chancery in Richmond. Also all estate right to any residents of persons wishing to purchase...Lewis Ensiminger...Ack'd 24 Jul 1829 in Monroe Co. by Henry Alexander and James Handley. Rec'd Oct 1829 Oliver Callaghan. Lifted by Damron 25 Nov 1830.

1:494 - 23 Sept 1829 - Elizabeth Morris's survey for her right of dower as widow of Archibald Morris. Land on Cedar Creek 53A with mill out of 169A. Land now claimed by George Mayse...William McClintic, Joseph Damron, and Robert Kincade commissioners appointed Dec 1828 to lay out dower. Rec'd Oct 1829 Oliver Callaghan.

1:495 - 14 Sept 1829 - William McCallister, Mary wife of Ross Co. OH appoint Joseph Damron as their attorney...William McCallister, Mary (X) McCallister...witness - M. Gillsillan, and William Kent...ack'd and cert'd in Ross Co. OH by William Gillsillan and Humphrey Fullerton. Rec'd Oct 1829 Oliver Callaghan. Lifted by Joeseph Damron Nov 1830.

1:496 - 14 Oct 1829 - Richard Snead, Nancy wife debtors, Charles L. Francisco and Henry M. Lewis trustees, Benjamin Thompson creditor.

Snead indebted to Thompson for $773.69 by bond Oct 1813., $1 paid by Francisco and Lewis for 450A in Bath Co. in Falling Spring Valley also for the following slaves, Jack 34 yrs. Milly 14 yrs. and Peter 2 yrs....neighbors - Anthony Mustoe, Lewis Payne, and John Couley...Richard Snead, Ann (^) Snead, Charles Francisco, Henry Lewis, Benjamin Thompson...witness - Francis Crutchfield, A. Sillington, Michael McClivce. Rec'd Oct 1829 Oliver Callaghan.

1:500 - 14 Apr 1818 - Decree of Chancery Court in Staunton 23 Jul 1808, James McElhiney plaintiff, Charles Rodgers, William Ward and Levi Skidmore defendants. Defendants make sale of certain lands in plaintiff's bill. Sold by Rodgers to Skidmore, also defendants 9 Sept 1813 at public auction sell 270A to Samuel Blackburn, agent of James McElhiney. Chancery Court held 8 Nov 1813 - defendents execute to plaintiff deed, the said deed not to affect claim of heirs of Josieh Lovjoy dec'd. THIS INDENTURE - 26 Jun 1816 - motion of plaintiff was ordered that Charles Francisco, John Lewis, and Andrew Warwick convey land to Benjamin Thompson...John Lewis, Andrew Warwick, Charles Francisco...ack'd in Bath Co. by Charles Francisco. Rec'd Oct 1829 Oliver Callaghan.

1:502 - THIS INDENTURE - Aug 1817 - William Podge of Bath Co. to Benjamin Thompson, $150 for his undivided two 5th's of 2 tracts. First tract 200A second tract 500A, both grants to Robert Armstrong Jr., 170A of last tract sold by Armstrong to John Eackman and 100A to George Hull, the residue being 350A...neighbor - McClintics...William Podge...ack'd in Bath Co. by Charles Francisco 12 Aug 1817. Rec'd Oct 1829 Oliver Callaghan.

1:504 - THIS INDENTURE - 17 Nov 1825 - John Morris of St. Charles in MO to Elizabeth Thompson, Charles T. Taylor and Sarah A. E. A. F. Taylor, all heirs of Benjamin Thomson, $100 paid for all right and title to several tracts of John Morris dec'd. John rec'd land from Richard Morris dec'd, one 10th part laid off by commissoner appointed at Chancery Court in Staunton, now depending in court by George W. Morris against others of Richard Morris dec'd...John Morris...witness - William Peters, Robert McClintic, William Millugton...ack'd in St. Charles MO by William G. Petty. Rec'd Oct 1829 Oliver Callaghan.

1:505 - THIS INDENTURE - 26 Apr 1824 - Nancy Lovjoy of Bath Co. to heirs of Benjamin Thomas dec'd. Josiah Lovjoy dec'd intestate leaving Nancy Lovjoy, Samuel Lovjoy and John Lovjoy his heirs. Nancy is entitled to one 3rd, $1 paid by heirs of Benjamin for her interest in one 3rd of 3 tracts. First 67A on Lick Run in Bath Co., part of 440A patent to James Armstrong. Second tract 200A, third tract 3? part of 270A was deeded to heirs, by Superior Court in Staunton 7 Nov 1818...Nancy Lovjoy...cert'd and ack'd in Bath Co. by William McClintic and Alexander McClintic 26 Apr 1824. Rec'd 12 Oct 1829 Oliver Callaghan.

1:508 - THIS INDENTURE - 25 Sept 1829 - John Delorum, Catherine wife to Samuel Kean both of Alleghany Co., $150 for 58A on Snake Run part of 400A granted James Thomas and joining the lands of George Carson and John Stone. Conveyed by James to John Delourm 3 Jun 1815. Also 100A on Snake Run part of 150A granted to John Delorum patent 29 Sept 1823, Tresuary warrant # 6182, and 50A of 150A...John (X)Delorum, Cathy (X) Delorum...release of dower, witnessed, and cert'd by John Callaghan and Sampson Sawyer. Rec'd Oct 1829 Oliver Callaghan. Lifted 15 Aug 1831 Samuel Kean Sr.

1:510 - THIS INDENTURE - 7 Oct 1829 - Stephen Hook Sr. to Elizabeth Hook and Daniel Hook, all of Alleghany Co., $1150 for 142A on Simpsons Creek, part of 300A surveyed for John Robinson and John Lewis 3 Apr 1746 vested in John Handley who conveyed to Peter Circle 6 Feb 1799, then conveyed by Andrew Circle, Elizabeth wife to Jacob Nicely, Magdalena wife. By them to Stephen Hook 24 Sept 1823, land on which he now lives...Stephen Hook Sr....witness - Joseph Damron, Conrad Lemon, Richard H. Wintz. Rec'd Oct 1829 Oliver Callaghan.

1:512 - 16 Oct 1829 - John Richardson, Mary wife debtors, William Terrill and George Payne trustees, George Sively creditor. John indebted to Sively for $190 by bond 16 Oct 1829. Terrill and Payne paid $1 for 55A first granted Moses Mann eldest son and heir of William Mann dec'd, patent 30 Apr 1795 vested in Richardson by sale from Moses. Also 150A granted Richardson by patent 22 Aug 1798 and

30A patented to Richardson 16 Sept 1808...John Richardson, Mary (X) Richardson, William Terrill, George Payne...release of dower by Jessis Davis and Samuel B. Lowrey. Rec'd Oct 1829 Oliver Callaghan. Lifted John Richardson 17 Mar 1835.

1:514 - Bond of Andrew Fudge, Charles Dressler, and William Terrill in the amount of $1,000. Condition is as such that Andrew Fudge is appointed a Commissioner of Public Revenue for the year of 1830...Andrew Fudge, Charles Dressler, William Terrill...ack'd by Fittius Turner.

20 Jan 1824 - Beniah Hutchinson on behalf of John Knox and William Knox infant heirs of John Knox dec'd and under 21 yrs., to Elisha Knox. Suit in Chancery 20 Oct 1823, Elisha plaintiff, infants and Hannah Knox defendants. Defendants convey to plaintiff deed with special warranty lands on Dunlaps Creek joining Bernard Pitzer. Land convey by Beniah Hutchinson. Rec'd 20 Jan 1824 Oliver Callaghan.

INDEX

----, Ama, 42
----, Charlotte, 42
----, D. P., 18
----, David S., 65
----, Elisha, 5
----, Elly, 42
----, Harrison, 78
----, Isabella, 79
----, Jack, 69, 84
----, John J., 33
----, Lewis, 65
----, Mariah, 31, 55
----, Mary, 48
----, Mary Jane, 38, 39
----, Michael, 19
----, Milly, 84
----, Nancy, 42
----, Patsy, 47, 70
----, Peter, 84
----, Prudence, 38
----, Rachael, 38, 39, 79
----, Sally, 47, 70
----, Williams, 48
ABRAHAM, Charles, 62-64
ABY, Polly S., 78
ALDERMEN, James McKeldal, 64
ALEXANDER, Henry, 17, 72, 83
ALLEN, James, 14
ALLEN, John, 5, 50
ALLEN, Kesiah, 66
ALLEN, Kesiah L., 66
ALLEN, Mounticue, 50, 66
AMEN, John, 38
ANDERSON, Catherine, 67
ANDERSON, Henry, 27, 62-64, 83
ANDERSON, John, 66
ANDERSON, John H., 74
ANDERSON, John T., 66, 67
ANDERSON, Robert, 33
ANDERSON, William, 31, 58
ARCHER, Branch T., 62
ARMENTROUT, 1, 22
ARMENTROUT, Catherine, 80
ARMENTROUT, David, 80
ARMENTROUT, Elizabeth, 42
ARMENTROUT, Frederick, 42
ARMENTROUT, George, 22, 60, 80
ARMENTROUT, Jacob, 9, 42
ARMESTEAD, John, 63
ARMISTEAD, John, 62, 64
ARMONTROUT, George, 18
ARMSTRONG, Archibald, 37, 38, 60
ARMSTRONG, Francis, 60, 61, 79
ARMSTRONG, James, 85
ARMSTRONG, John, 60
ARMSTRONG, Nancy, 60
ARMSTRONG JR., Robert, 37, 84
ARRITT, John, 16, 21, 29, 32, 35, 42, 66-68, 74-76, 79, 80
ARRITT, Michael, 4, 5, 8, 11, 16, 21, 32, 35, 42, 66-68, 76, 80
AUFRYNOSE, Lewis Phillibert Brun, 61, 63
AUFRYNOSE, Lewis Phillibert Brund, 63
AUGUSTUS, John, 8
BALWIN, Charles, 73
BANKS, Henry, 62, 63
BARKER, John, 58
BARLING, Joseph, 55

BAUGHMAN, Christopher, 2
BEAL, John, 44, 45
BEIME, Andrew, 30, 33
BEIME, Andrew Jr., 30
BEIME, George, 30, 33
BEIME, Isaac, 30
BEIME, Polly, 30
BELL, H., 55
BELL, Jereamiah B., 18
BENNETT, Jacob, 9
BENNETT, Joseph, 6
BENNETT, Mary, 9
BENSON, Andrien, 73
BENSON, Babel, 73
BERNARD, Allen, 53
BERRS, Andres, 62
BESS, Henry, 47
BESS, William, 47
BEVERLY, William, 10, 23, 73
BISHOP, Abraham, 26, 27
BLACKBURN, Samuel, 84
BLAIR, Alexander, 13, 34
BOLLAR, John, 37
BOSWELL, John, 48, 52, 80
BOSWELL, John H., 64
BOSWELL, John L., 35, 37, 44, 47, 49, 50, 52, 53, 59, 80
BOSWELL, John P., 83
BOWYER, David, 4, 80
BOWYER, H. W., 37
BOWYER, John M., 79
BOYCE, John, 53
BOYLE, Hugh, 8
BRADLEY, John, 65
BRATTON, Robert, 41, 50, 61
BRECKENRIDGE, James, 18, 36, 37, 54

BRICE, Nicholas, 56, 57
BRIGHT, David, 43
BROOKE, Robert, 70
BROOKS, Catherine, 46
BROOKS, Lasson, 46
BROOKS, Robert, 70
BROWN, *, 2, 19, 67, 68
BROWN, Francis, 60
BROWN, James, 10, 26, 27, 47, 48, 74
BROWN, John, 18
BROWN, John, 67
BROWN, Mathew, 18
BROWN, Mathew D., 18
BROWN, Samuel, 1, 2, 5, 8, 9, 13, 26, 27, 40, 44, 60
BROWN, William, 18, 67
BROWN JR., Samuel, 31
BRUNNEMER, Anthony, 13, 71
BRUNNEMER, Joanah, 25
BRUNNEMER, John, 25, 39
BRUNNEMER, Manza Jane, 25
BRUNNEMER JR., John, 42
BULLACK, David, 54
BURD, Mary, 53
BURD, William, 43, 53
BURK, James, 3, 7, 8, 9, 24
BUSH, Nathan, 78, 79
BUTCHER, 1
BUTCHER, Jacob, 1, 34
BUTCHER, Nancy, 1, 8
BUTCHER SR., Jacob, 1
BUZZARD, Hannah, 2, 28
BUZZARD, Leonard, 2, 28
BYRD, Dianah, 38, 45
BYRD, Dianna, 38
BYRD, Elizabeth, 38, 39
BYRD, Thomas, 5, 9, 11, 13, 32, 35, 38, 43, 45, 50, 51

BYRD SR., John, 38, 39
CAFIELD, Edward D., 58
CALHOUN, Robert, 45
CALL, John, 9
CALLAGHAN, 12
CALLAGHAN, Agnes, 13
CALLAGHAN, Charles, 2-5, 7, 13, 15, 17, 20, 24-27, 30, 34-36, 45, 52, 64, 68, 70, 71
CALLAGHAN, D., 2, 6, 18, 20, 43, 71, 73
CALLAGHAN, Dennis, 20, 26, 59
CALLAGHAN, Elvira W., 59, 10
CALLAGHAN, John, 1, 2, 4, 5, 8, 9, 11-13, 15, 17, 24, 26-28, 30, 35, 36, 38, 46, 51, 52, 55, 59, 64, 68, 76, 77, 85
CALLAGHAN, Julia, 20
CALLAGHAN, Margaret, 59
CALLAGHAN, Nancy, 13
CALLAGHAN, Olive, 57
CALLAGHAN, Oliver, 1-26, 28-49, 51-61, 64-86
CALLAGHAN, William, 2, 28, 33, 34, 46
CAPIDY, Charlotte, 58
CARPENTER, Samuel, 28
CARPERTON, Thomas H., 8
CARPERTON, Thompson H., 7
CARRIGAN, Jacob, 23
CARRIGAN, Mary, 23
CARRIGAN, Michael, 23
CARRIGAN, Patrick, 23
CARRINGTON, Richard A., 7, 8
CARSON, Geoge, 57

CARSON, George, 37, 53, 57, 85
CARSON, John A., 3
CARSON, Matilda C., 53, 57
CARTER, John, 62
CARY, William, 59
CAVENDER, Alice, 16
CAVENDISH, 37
CAVENDISH, Alice, 14
CHAMBERS, George, 39
CHANDLER, R. M., 35
CHENT, Henry B., 56
CHRISTIAN, Saluda B., 22
CHRISTIAN, William H. B., 21, 22
CIRCLE, Andrew, 14, 16, 85
CIRCLE, Elizabeth, 14, 16, 85
CIRCLE, George, 22
CIRCLE, Lewis, 16
CIRCLE, Magdalena, 14
CIRCLE, Martha L., 16
CIRCLE, Peter, 14, 16, 22, 85
CLARK, Christina, 81
CLARK, Christine, 81
CLARK, George, 53
CLARK, Joseph B., 72, 73, 81
CLARK, William, 73
CLAYPOOL, George, 13
CLAYTON, Samuel, 53, 54
CLEAR, Jacob, 52
CLEAR, Susannah, 52
CLENDENEN, James, 49, 58
CLENDENEN, Sally, 49, 58
CLINTUK, James M., 41
COALTER, Robert, 30, 33
COHERD, Henry B., 56
COLLINS, Hale, 28
CONNER, Henry, 10, 74

COOK, John, 7, 74
CORVLING, William, 64
COULEY, John, 84
COWAN, William, 53
COX, James, 14, 16
COX, Nathan, 67
COX, William, 67
CRAIN, John, 71
CRAWFORD, 15, 18
CRAWFORD, Andrew, 14
CRAWFORD, John, 70
CRAWFORD, Robert, 14
CRAWFORD, Samuel, 14
CRAWFORD, Thomas, 6
CRAWFORD, William, 6
CREASON, John, 43
CROW, John, 2, 6, 8, 9, 27, 31, 34, 38, 58, 61
CROW, Joseph, 38
CRUTCHFIELD, A., 39
CRUTCHFIELD, Benjamin T. B., 38, 39
CRUTCHFIELD, Francis, 39, 47, 51, 54, 70, 84
CRUTCHFIELD, John M. D., 39
CRUTCHFIELD, Thomas, 49
CUMMINGS, A., 75
CUMMINGS, Absalom, 66, 68, 75
CUMMINGS, Catherine, 66
CUMMINGS, Hugh, 66, 68
CUMMINGS, Rebecca, 68
CUMP, D. P., 18
DAGGER, Peter, 72
DAMRON, Andrew, 76
DAMRON, Christopher, 76
DAMRON, John, 6, 8, 10, 15, 34, 43, 76
DAMRON, Joseph, 25, 29,
DAMRON, Joseph (Cont.) 30, 33, 34, 41-48, 51, 55, 59-61, 65, 67-69, 71, 76, 77, 82, 83, 85
DAMRON, Polly, 15
DAMRON, William, 76
DAMRON SR., John, 76
DAUGHTRY, Thomas, 41
DAVAL, William, 21
DAVID, Thomas, 66
DAVIES, Augustine, 53
DAVIS, Jesse, 5
DAVIS, Jessie, 13, 21, 24, 34, 45, 61, 64, 86
DAVIS, Samuel, 42
DAVIS, Thomas, 20, 36, 77
DAVIS, William H., 25
DAWSON, John, 63
DEAN, William, 43
DEEDS, John, 5, 15
DELORN, Catherine, 37
DELORN, John, 37
DELORUM, Catherine, 85
DELORUM, Cathy, 85
DELORUM, John, 85
DELOURM, John, 85
DEW, Achilles, 16
DEW, Archilles, 16
DEW, Charles, 76
DEW, Nancy, 76
DEW, Samuel, 76
DEW, William, 3, 8, 9, 42
DICKERSON, John, 65
DISCON, Thomas, 22
DODGE, Hazekiak, 78
DONNALLY, 29
DOUGLAS, B. T., 73
DOUGLAS, Ben R., 20
DOUGLAS, Benjamin, 64, 66
DOUGLAS, Benjamin T., 18,

DOUGLAS, Benj. T. (Cont.) 43, 71
DRESSLER, 13
DRESSLER, Absolom, 17
DRESSLER, Absolum, 6
DRESSLER, Adam, 5, 9, 17, 35, 82
DRESSLER, Barbara, 17
DRESSLER, Barbary, 6
DRESSLER, Charles, 6, 9, 17, 35, 82, 83, 86
DRESSLER, Charlotte, 17
DRESSLER, Elizabeth, 24, 46, 59, 74, 81, 82, 83
DRESSLER, George, 74, 81, 82
DRESSLER, Henry, 5, 17, 24, 26, 35, 39, 46-48, 51, 59, 71, 72, 81-83
DRESSLER, Jacob, 10, 81, 82
DRESSLER, John, 6, 17
DRESSLER, Malinda, 6, 35, 81, 82
DRESSLER, Margaret, 81
DRESSLER, Margaret Ann, 82
DRESSLER, Martha, 5, 17
DRESSLER, Mary, 47
DRESSLER, Michael, 47
DRESSLER, Milinda, 17
DRESSLER, Moses, 26, 47, 81, 82
DRESSLER, Peter, 5, 17, 35
DRESSLER, Sally, 5, 35
DRESSLER, Sarah, 17
DRESSLER, William, 2, 81, 82
DRESSLERS, Henry, 25
DREW, Peyton, 58
DRUMOND, George, 20, 21

DUDDING, John, 78, 79
DUDDING, Rebecca, 78, 79
DUKE, Hugh, 68, 78, 81
DUNLAP, Alexander, 76, 77
DUNLAP, David, 79
DUVAL, Phillip, 22
DUVAL, William, 22
DYER, William, 19
EACKMAN, John, 84
EAKINS, Nathan, 7
EASTHAM, Robert, 34
EDGAR, David, 59
EHSENNEH, Jean Sigismond, 61, 63
ELLIOT, Isabella, 40, 41
ELLIOT, William, 40, 41
ENSIMINGER, Lewis, 61, 62, 63, 64, 83
ENSIMINGER, Lewis L., 83
ERSKINE, Henry, 36
ERSKINE, Michael, 19, 61
ESTER, George, 81, 82
ESTHRIDGE, William S., 70
EXERSTACE, John H., 8
EXERSTANCE, John H., 8
FACHETT, Nimrod, 3
FAIRFAX, Ferdenando, 4
FAUGHT, George, 42, 78, 79
FAUGHT, John, 42
FAUGHT, Margaret (Polly), 79
FAUGHT, Polly, 78
FAULKNER, A. M., 41, 78
FEHNWICK, William, 53
FENWICK, William, 53, 54
FIGGOT, Henry, 5
FIKE, Able, 35
FISHER, Phillip, 18, 19, 67
FLEAGE, Jacob, 6
FLEET, 3
FLEET, Alexander, 3, 17, 44

FLEET, Elizabeth, 3
FLOOD, Henry, 22
FOSTER, Druna, 18
FOSTER, Francis, 2, 28, 41, 69, 72
FOSTER, Nancy, 28
FOSTER, Sally, 18
FOSTER, Sarah, 18
FOWLER, Owens C., 22
FRALEY, Adam, 4
FRANCIS, John, 53
FRANCISCO, Charles, 84
FRANCISCO, Charles L., 24, 29, 83, 84
FRAZER, Addison, 31, 43, 51, 59
FRAZER, James, 31, 32
FRIDLEY, Charles, 45
FUDGE, 82
FUDGE, Andrew, 47, 58, 68, 81, 86
FUDGE, Conrad, 25, 33, 39, 48, 74, 82
FUDGE, Elizabeth, 74, 82
FUDGE, Jacob, 24, 47
FULLERTON, Humphrey, 41, 83
FULTON, Alexander, 54
FURWELL, James, 28
GANTS, James, 20
GARLAND, David S., 55
GIBSON, Jane, 75
GIBSON, Lyndia, 75
GIBSON, Patrick, 53
GIBSON, Thomas M., 75
GIBSON, William, 55- 57
GILES, William, 68
GILES, William B., 58
GILLASPIE, 21
GILLASPIE, Comfort, 58
GILLASPIE, Elizabeth, 45

GILLASPIE, James H., 43, 44, 45
GILLASPIE, John, 44, 58, 66, 67
GILLASPIE, Nancy, 67
GILLASPIE, Rebecca, 67
GILLASPIE, Simon, 43, 44, 45, 66, 67
GILLASPIE, William, 29
GILLESPIE, William, 29
GILLILAND, James, 28, 45, 80
GILLILAND, John B., 78
GILLILAND, Mary, 80
GILLSILLAN, M., 83
GILLSILLAN, William, 83
GLASSBURN, David, 69
GLASSBURN, Frederick, 69
GLASSBURNS, David, 69
GORDON, Robert, 53
GORES, Michael, 58
GOSHEN, Mark H., 40, 41
GRAF, John, 28
GRAF, Peter, 28
GRAHAM, 29
GRAMER, Joseph, 42
GRAMMARS, Joseph, 68
GRAP, Mary, 9
GRAP, Peter, 9
GRAP JR., Peter, 9
GRAY, Isaac, 18, 68
GRAY, Lucy, 68, 77
GREENWOOD, Henry B., 9
GREENWOOD, Henry Bailey, 38
GREENWOOD, Nancy, 38
GREETING, Jean Mathias, 61, 63, 64
GREIGH, Thomas, 69
GRIFFIN, John G., 2
GRIFFITH, 67

GRIFFITH, Comfort, 58
GRIFFITH, Elizabeth, 49, 58
GRIFFITH, Lucy, 14, 18, 49, 58, 60
GRIFFITH, Mary, 58, 59
GRIFFITH, Nancy, 49, 58
GRIFFITH, Orlando, 14, 18, 49, 58, 60
GRIFFITH, Sally, 49, 58
GRIFFITH, William, 49, 58
GROSE, Nancy, 75, 76
GROSE, Samuel, 75, 76
GROVER, Josiah, 78, 79
GULLY, Mary, 58
HALE, Alexander S., 50
HAMILL, Joseph, 78
HAMILTON, Andrew, 2, 6, 25
HANCE, Boston, 67
HANDLEY, James, 30, 72, 83
HANDLEY, John, 14
HANDLEY, John, 16
HANDLEY, John, 85
HANK, 7
HANK, David, 3, 8, 24, 30
HANLEY, James, 17, 33
HANNA, David, 61, 64
HANSBARGER, Boston, 16
HANSBARGER, Elizabeth, 25
HANSBARGER, Jacob, 20, 23, 25
HANSBARGER, John, 20, 25, 45
HANSBARGER, Sebastian, 15, 20, 25
HANSBARGER SR., John, 25
HANSBRGER, 44
HANSFORD, Felix, 47
HANSFORD, Felix G., 32
HANSFORD, Sarah, 32, 47
HANSFORD, Sarah K., 32
HANSON, Charles W., 56, 57
HANSON, James, 50
HARDING, William, 10
HARDY, Ann, 15
HARDY, Barkely, 15
HARDY, Becky, 15
HARDY, Berkely, 68
HARDY, Elizabeth, 9, 10, 76
HARDY, George, 15, 18, 77
HARDY, Jacob, 15
HARDY, John, 9, 10, 15, 33, 41, 48, 59, 76, 77
HARDY, Polly, 15
HARDY, Rebecca, 15
HARDY, Samuel, 15
HARDY, Sarah, 15
HARDY, Thomas, 10, 15
HARDY, William, 15, 77
HARMON, Andrew, 50
HARMON, Anthony, 50
HARMON, Christopher, 69, 72
HARMON, George, 39
HARNSBARGER, Boston, 14
HARRISON, Mieajah, 43, 45
HARTMAN, J., 22
HARTMAN, John, 10
HARVEY, Mathew, 54
HARVEY, Robert, 21
HAWKINS, John, 30
HAWS, W., 19
HAY, John, 35
HAYNES, Benjamin, 3, 34, 44, 48, 51, 59
HAYNES, William H., 2, 10, 13, 14, 20, 25, 46, 52, 60

HEAFORD, William A., 77
HEATH, James, 61
HEATH, James E., 61, 63
HEATH, T., 55
HELMINTOLLER, 59
HELMINTOLLER, Palser, 64, 65
HELMINTOLLER, Peter, 57
HENING, William W., 62
HERBERT, William, 1, 2, 4-6, 8, 9, 15, 31, 34, 47, 55
HERFORD, William A., 66
HILL, William, 1
HINCHMON, John, 74
HITE, Rachael, 34
HITE, William, 34
HOBBS, James, 73
HOLLOWAY, J. H., 18
HOLLOWAY, John, 2, 4, 5, 10, 13, 14, 15, 20, 21, 64, 69, 77, 78
HOLLOWAY, William, 2, 47-51, 55, 59, 77
HOLLOWAY, William G., 18, 42, 48, 49, 50, 51
HOLLOWELL, John, 55-58
HOLLOWELL, Mary, 58
HOLLOWELL, Rebecca, 55, 58
HOLLY, David, 29
HOLLY, Elon, 11, 61, 64
HOLLY, John A., 11, 40, 61, 64
HOOK, Daniel, 85
HOOK, Eli, 14, 16
HOOK, Elizabeth, 85
HOOK, Stephen, 11, 14, 18, 85
HOOK SR., Stephen, 85
HOOKS, Stephen, 9, 20, 36, 42, 45, 50, 64, 68, 77

HOUSTON, Mathew, 53
HOWARD, John, 16
HULL, George, 84
HULL, Henry, 19
HUMPHRIES, Jessie, 30, 68, 69
HUMPHRIES, Sarah, 4
HUMPHRIES, Uriah, 4, 65
HUMPHRIES, William, 13, 29, 68
HUNTER, Joseph, 4
HUNTER, William, 47, 61, 71
HUTCHINSON, Archibald, 14
HUTCHINSON, Beniah, 14, 21, 86
HUTCHINSON, George, 53
HUTCHINSON, Isaac, 30
HYLSEY, 37
IRVINE, John, 55, 56
IRVINE, Selina, 56
IRVINE, Selina Ann, 56
IRWIN, 21
IRWIN, Samuel, 20, 81
ISRAEL, Fielder, 55
JACKSON, Jane, 40
JARVIS, Zoper, 4
JEROME, Charles William Jeste, 63
JEROME, Charles William Juste, 61, 63
JOHNSON, Hyriam, 31
JOHNSON, Isaac, 1, 20, 27
JOHNSON, J., 27
JOHNSON, John, 31, 32, 36, 66, 70, 77
JOHNSON, Susanna, 21
JOHNSON, William, 21, 31, 32
JOHNSTON, 80

JOHNSTON, Eve, 28, 32
JOHNSTON, George, 41
JOHNSTON, Isaac, 1
JOHNSTON, John, 44, 45
JOHNSTON, Susannah, 32
JOHNSTON, William, 32, 36
JONES, Loviah, 38, 47, 76
JONES, Oliver L., 60
JONES, Valentine, 38, 47, 76
JONES, Vanlentine, 41
JONES, Wharton, 75
JONES, William R., 3, 6, 7, 25, 46
JORDAN, Edward, 56
JORDAN, F., 46
JORDAN, H., 56
JORDAN, John, 55-57
JORDAN, Lucy, 56
JORDAN, Samuel F., 56
JORDAY, John, 46
KARNES, Elizabeth, 79
KARNES, George, 79
KARNES, James, 6
KARNES, James, 32, 49, 53, 70, 71, 80
KARNES, Thomas, 28, 74
KARNES JR., James, 50
KARNS, James, 8, 50
KEAN, D., 35
KEAN, David, 6, 13, 38, 61
KEAN, Elizabeth, 61
KEAN, Lucy, 30, 38
KEAN, Samuel, 34, 37, 38, 42, 43, 51, 85
KEAN JR., Samuel, 59
KEAN SR., Samuel, 44, 59, 85
KEANS, James, 3, 23
KEARNS, Jane, 35, 36
KEARNS, Thomas, 35, 36
KELLY, 68

KELLY, Thomas, 56
KELSO, Robert, 2, 22, 70-74
KELSO, Susanna, 7
KENT, William, 83
KERLY, John A., 66
KERR, 65
KERR, Alexander M., 4
KERR, George, 4
KEYSER, Fleming, 60, 61, 79
KEYSER, James D., 18
KEYSER, Joseph, 6
KEYSER, Joseph D., 3-5, 7, 8, 14-17, 20, 25, 35, 43, 46, 52, 60, 66, 71, 73
KEYSER, Margaret, 40
KEYSER, Nancy, 60, 61
KIBBLE, James, 69
KIMBERLINE, 42
KIMBERLINE, Dianah, 8
KIMBERLINE, Diannah, 8
KIMBERLINE, Elizabeth Ann, 11, 35
KIMBERLINE, Francis, 49, 50
KIMBERLINE, Henry, 49, 68, 77
KIMBERLINE, Jacob, 45, 49, 68, 77
KIMBERLINE, James, 8, 9, 11, 35
KIMBERLINE, John, 8
KIMBERLINE, Jonathan, 4, 8
KIMBERLINE, Joseph, 42
KIMBERLINE, Lorenzo, 11
KIMBERLINE, Lorezo D., 35
KIMBERLINE, Maria, 42
KIMBERLINE, Michael, 15, 42, 50, 68

KIMBERLINE, Nancy, 4, 8, 11, 35
KIMBERLINE, Rinehard, 49, 50
KIMBERLINE, Washington, 11, 35
KIMBERLINE, William, 35
KINCADE, Andrew, 16, 17
KINCADE, Ann, 17
KINCADE, Archibald M., 33
KINCADE, James, 16, 17
KINCADE, Phebe, 16, 17
KINCADE, Robert, 2, 4, 5, 8, 9, 16, 17, 33, 83
KINCADE, William, 17
KINCAID, A. M., 41
KINCAID, Andrew, 40, 48
KINCAID, Archibald, 67
KINCAID, Archibald M., 67
KINCAID, James, 38
KINCAID, Mary, 48
KINCAID, Robert, 21, 35, 67
KINCAID, Thomas, 48
KINCAID, William, 29
KINDELL, James, 31
KING, Isbella, 79
KING, John, 79
KIRKPATRICK, Thomas, 38, 61, 64
KNIGHT, George, 24
KNOOTZ, Michael, 66
KNOX, 12
KNOX, Agnes, 82
KNOX, Charles, 11
KNOX, Elisha, 3, 5, 7, 11, 17, 21, 23, 73, 74, 82, 86
KNOX, Hannah, 21, 86
KNOX, James, 26, 27, 29, 50
KNOX, John, 11, 21, 82, 86
KNOX, Nelson, 21
KNOX, Oliver, 11
KNOX, Reubin, 59
KNOX, Susan, 65
KNOX, William, 11-13, 21, 65, 86
KNOX JR., Elisha, 7, 11, 23, 71
KNOX SR., Elisha, 17, 65, 71
KNOXS, James, 26
KYLE, 80
KYLE, Agnes, 47
KYLE, William, 32, 47, 51, 53, 69, 73, 75
LATHAM, Henry, 78
LATHAM, Polly S., 78
LATHAM, Silas, 81
LATHAM, Silas G., 24, 25
LAW, Jacob A., 74
LAYNE, Douglas B., 74
LECLERVY, Francis, 13
LEGRAND, Nash, 3, 7, 10, 46, 49
LEMERCIER, Henry, 61, 63, 64
LEMON, Conrad, 14, 52, 85
LEMON, George, 14, 15, 16
LEMON, Nancy, 15
LEWIS, 43, 45
LEWIS, Andrew, 29
LEWIS, Benjamin, 24
LEWIS, General, 34
LEWIS, Henry, 84
LEWIS, Henry M., 83, 84
LEWIS, John, 14, 16, 41, 60, 84, 85
LEWIS, Joseph, 11
LEWIS, Samuel, 29
LIGHTNER, Nathan, 23
LINCH, Hugh, 35
LINGLANGHER, John, 44

LINGLOCKER, Archibald, 45
LINKHORNS, 29
LITTLEPAGE, James B., 32, 46
LITTLEPAGE, R., 45
LITTLEPAGE, William, 32, 46
LITTLEPAGE, William S., 46
LOCKHART, David, 26, 31, 34
LOCKHART, Elizabeth, 40
LOCKHARTS, David, 26
LOGUE, Samuel, 4, 41
LONG, John, 26, 27
LONG, Robert, 56, 57
LONG, Sarah, 57
LORMON, William, 57
LOVJOY, John, 85
LOVJOY, Josiah, 85
LOVJOY, Josieh, 84
LOVJOY, Nancy, 85
LOVJOY, Samuel, 85
LOWERY, Samuel B., 22, 47, 49, 50, 52, 59, 72, 75, 76, 79, 80, 82, 83, 86
LUDINGTON, Francis, 31, 51, 59
MADDON, Warner, 78
MADISON, J. C., 2
MAGGARD, Adam, 19
MAGGARD, David, 19
MAGGARD, Joseph, 19
MAGGARD SR., David, 19
MALL, Jacob, 57
MALL, Jacob S., 57
MALLOW, Catherine, 13, 25, 26
MALLOW, Cathy, 13
MALLOW, Christina, 28, 39
MALLOW, George, 9, 22, 25, 26, 28, 33, 47, 68, 74, 83
MALLOW, Jacob, 13
MALLOW, John, 13, 25, 68
MALLOW, Michael, 13, 20, 25, 28, 39, 69
MALLOW, W., 1
MALLOW SR., Michael, 25
MANN, 11
MANN, Archibald, 5, 14, 40, 65, 70, 75, 76
MANN, Elizabeth, 7
MANN, Francis, 54
MANN, Hamilton, 5, 6, 7, 10, 40, 65, 66, 70, 75
MANN, Jane, 75
MANN, John, 5, 14, 40, 70, 75
MANN, John M. D., 65
MANN, Lewis, 40, 66, 70
MANN, Lewis L., 75
MANN, Lewis T., 20, 65
MANN, Margaret, 14, 15
MANN, Mary, 66
MANN, Moses, 1, 5, 14, 21, 22, 40, 54, 70, 80, 85
MANN, Moses H., 1, 2, 5, 9, 10, 11, 16, 17, 22, 24, 31, 48, 51, 67
MANN, Sally, 5
MANN, Sarah, 40, 52, 65
MANN, William, 5, 20, 22, 40, 67, 85
MANN, William T., 14, 15
MANN JR., Moses, 1
MANN SR., Moses, 1, 11, 71
MARMUNDO, Charles J., 53
MASSIE, Henry, 21, 70
MATHENY, 32
MATHENY, Jane, 36

MATHENY, Rebecca, 25, 36
MATHENY, Samuel, 74
MATHENY, William, 25, 31, 36
MATHERNY, William, 25
MAYO, Phillip, 53, 54
MAYSE, George, 83
MC? SR., Thomas, 72
MCALISTER, Hugh, 62
MCALLISTER, John, 22
MCCALLISTER, 2
MCCALLISTER, Andrew, 80
MCCALLISTER, Barbara, 80
MCCALLISTER, James, 31, 34, 43, 71, 76
MCCALLISTER, John, 48, 71, 80
MCCALLISTER, Mary, 48, 83
MCCALLISTER, Samuel, 34, 43, 71, 76
MCCALLISTER, Thomas, 80
MCCALLISTER, William, 29, 48, 65, 83
MCCALLISTER JR., William, 48
MCCALLISTERS, Barbara, 48
MCCAUSLAND, John, 29
MCCLELLAND, John, 56
MCCLINTIC, 84
MCCLINTIC, Alex, 2, 14
MCCLINTIC, Alexander, 33, 37, 73, 85
MCCLINTIC, Alexander H., 33
MCCLINTIC, James W., 14
MCCLINTIC, Jane, 75

MCCLINTIC, John, 75
MCCLINTIC, Moses, 28, 33, 73, 75
MCCLINTIC, Robert, 28, 73, 75, 84
MCCLINTIC, Sarah, 14, 75
MCCLINTIC, Sarah W., 14
MCCLINTIC, William, 15, 24, 33, 38, 45, 61, 83, 85
MCCLIVCE, Michael, 84
MCCLUNG, William, 29
MCCOLLISTER, Mary, 47, 48
MCCOLLISTER, Polly, 48
MCCOLLISTER, William, 48
MCCOLLISTER JR., William, 47
MCCRUMB, Robert, 38, 45
MCDANIEL, Albon, 53
MCDEAN, William, 15, 38, 45
MCDONALD, W., 41
MCDOWELL, William A., 2
MCELHINEY, James, 84
MCKINSEY, Samuel, 33
MCLAUGHLIN, James, 15, 31
MCMAHON, John J., 30
MCMECHEN, William, 55
MCMILLEN, Ed, 13
MCMULLIN, Edward, 38, 76, 82
MCMULLIN, Jane, 76
MCMULLIN, Joseph, 76
MCMULLIN, Samuel, 34
MCPHERSON, Christopher, 21, 22
MCPHILLIP, Alex, 29
MEAD, Hiram N., 41

MERRY, James, 1-3, 6-8, 10-12, 15, 18, 20, 22-24, 28-34, 36-41, 43, 47-49, 51, 52, 65, 70-74
MERRY, Kelso, 74
MERRY, Mary, 3, 6-8, 10-12, 18, 20, 22-24, 28, 38, 40, 41, 43, 49, 52, 70, 71
MERRY, Mary R., 8, 18, 22, 24, 28, 32, 37, 41, 49, 71, 72, 73
MERRY, Samauel, 70
MERRY, Samuel, 3, 6-8, 10-12, 18, 20, 22, 37, 43, 70-74
METHANEY, Rebecca, 77
MEYER, Henry, 66, 68
MEYERS, George, 17, 33, 71, 72
MEYERS, Katherine, 17
MEYERS SR., George, 72
MILLER, Daniel, 31
MILLER, T. B., 2
MILLHOLLIN, Patrick, 3, 8, 18, 22, 24, 25, 33, 77
MILLUGTON, William, 84
MINCHIE, John, 53
MOFFETT, H. M., 29
MOORE, Andrew, 4
MOORE, John, 79
MOORE, Stephen, 18
MOOSMAN, John I., 66
MORGAN, William, 22
MORGON, William H., 30
MORRIS, Ann, 41
MORRIS, Archibald, 10, 31, 43, 51, 54, 60, 83
MORRIS, Benjamin, 41, 51, 60
MORRIS, Elizabeth, 31, 51, 54, 83

MORRIS, Francis, 60, 61
MORRIS, G. W., 79
MORRIS, George W., 84
MORRIS, George Washington, 60, 79
MORRIS, Isabella, 41
MORRIS, John, 40, 84
MORRIS, Nancy, 60
MORRIS, Richard, 40, 41, 60, 61, 79, 84
MORRIS, William, 40, 41
MORRIS SR., Richard, 51
MORRISON, Fountain, 49
MORTON, Catherine, 69
MORTON, William F., 39, 44, 69
MOYER, George, 46, 47, 61, 65
MOYER, Rosannah, 61
MOYER SR., George, 46, 47, 48, 61
MOYERS SR., George, 47
MULLHOLLIN, Thomas, 39
MUSTOE, Anthony, 84
MYER, Samuel, 57
NEAL, Alice, 34
NEAL, Hugh, 43
NEAL, Hugh N., 34
NEAL, John, 34, 42
NEAL, Polly, 34
NEAL, Rebecca, 34, 42, 43
NEAL SR., John, 34, 43
NEECE, Jacob, 2
NELSON, Alexander, 33
NEVILLE, Maria, 83
NEVILLE, Samuel, 82, 83
NEWELL, John, 18
NEWELL, Nancy, 44, 67
NEWELL, Thomas, 44, 45, 66, 67
NICELY, Andrew, 16

NICELY, Betsy, 46
NICELY, J., 16
NICELY, Jacob, 14, 16, 46, 85
NICELY, Louis Jacob, 16
NICELY, Magdalane, 16
NICELY, Magdalena, 14, 16, 85
NICHOLAS, Henry, 33
NORTH, Abraham K., 53
NORTH, John A., 40
OGDAN, Joseph, 57
OGDEN, Joseph I., 56
ORR, Benjamin Grayson, 63
PAINTURF, Jacob, 37
PARKER, Hugh, 65
PARKER, Jeremiah, 56, 58
PARKER, Margaret, 65, 82
PARKER, Richard, 56, 58
PARKER, William, 58
PARRIS, Alexander, 51, 54, 60, 61
PARRIS, Benjamin, 62
PARRIS, Ellen, 54
PATTERSON, 50
PATTERSON, Elizabeth, 68
PATTERSON, William, 42, 68
PAYNE, George, 85, 86
PAYNE, George H., 22, 55, 57, 58, 73, 78
PAYNE, Lewis, 84
PENCE, Betsy, 37
PENCE, Elizabeth, 37, 57
PENCE, Henry, 81, 82
PENCE, Peter, 4, 5, 8, 9, 13, 15, 18, 20, 22, 25, 31, 36, 37, 45, 50, 53, 57, 66, 72, 77
PENDLETON, William G., 63

PENLYING, George, 22
PENNINGTON, Josiah, 57
PEROT, Francis Joseph, 61, 64
PERSINGER, 21
PERSINGER, Adam, 78, 79
PERSINGER, Andrew, 3, 34, 45
PERSINGER, Barbara, 78, 79
PERSINGER, Barbary, 78
PERSINGER, Charlotte, 79
PERSINGER, Christopher, 29, 78, 79
PERSINGER, George, 78, 79
PERSINGER, Griselda, 16
PERSINGER, Henry, 9, 16
PERSINGER, Jacob, 2, 3, 7, 16, 24, 29, 30, 42, 78, 79
PERSINGER, John, 3, 11, 13, 15, 29, 34, 51, 64-66, 68, 74-76, 79, 80
PERSINGER, Lee, 3, 24
PERSINGER, Margaret, 16, 78, 79
PERSINGER, Moses, 3, 4, 6, 8, 24, 71, 79
PERSINGER, Rachael, 79
PERSINGER, Sampson, 42
PERSINGER, William, 78, 79
PERSINGER SR., Jacob, 19, 69
PETER, William G., 42
PETERS, William, 84
PETTY, William G., 84
PEYTON, John, 21
PEYTON, John H., 24, 40, 70
PICKERING, Sam, 56
PICKERING, Samuel, 56
PINNELL, Harriet, 15, 16

PINNELL, Joseph, 15, 16, 71
PITZER, 66
PITZER, A. B., 10
PITZER, Abraham, 10
PITZER, Barnard, 2, 31
PITZER, Bernard, 21, 31, 72, 80, 86
PITZER, Davidson, 5
PITZER, Duiguid, 72
PITZER, Jane, 71, 72
PITZER, John, 15, 21
PITZER, Joseph K., 72
PITZER, Madison, 6
PITZER, Mary, 10
PITZER, Sally, 72
PITZER, Sarah, 72
PLEASANT JR., James, 13
PLEASANTS, A., 49
PLEASANTS, James, 33, 34
PODGE, William, 84
POGUE SR., Samuel, 10, 76
PORTER, 21
PORTER, Samuel, 15, 50
PORTER, Sarah, 15
PORTER, William R., 3, 6, 7, 25, 46
PRABOW, H. P., 58
PRABOW, Henry, 58
PRICE, William, 63
PUKERING, Abraham, 8
PUROT, Joseph, 63
PUTNAM, John, 29
QUARRIEN, Alexander W., 79
QUICKLE, Adam, 81, 82
QUICKLE, Margaret, 81
QUICKLE, Mary, 81
QUINN, John, 59
RAGLAND, James, 27, 60
RAGLAND, James P., 60, 61
RAMSEY, 4
RAMSEY, E., 10
RAMSEY, Edmond, 4
RANDALPH, Thomas M., 1
RANDOLPH, Peyton, 54
RAWLINGS, James, 49
RAYHILL, Alexander, 16
RAYHILL, Ester, 18, 67
RAYHILL, George, 34, 35
READER, George, 30
REDEM, Count of, 63
REDERN, Count of, 61, 62, 63, 64
REED, Archibald, 20, 21
REED, John, 55
REED, John A., 29, 55
REED, Susanna, 20, 21
REES, David, 4
REES, Eleanor, 9
REES, John, 9, 10, 41
REESE, John, 76, 77
REID, 45
REID, John, 61
REID, John A., 29, 61, 64
REIGART, John, 23
RETOWELL, George, 30, 31, 32, 46, 55
REYNOLDS, Obadiah, 25
RICE, Anna, 71
RICE, Mathew, 53
RICE, Mathew H., 53
RICE, William, 71
RICHARDS, Walter, 29
RICHARDSON, 86
RICHARDSON, Elizabeth, 21
RICHARDSON, John, 35, 49, 65, 66, 85, 86
RICHARDSON, Margaret, 21
RICHARDSON, Mary, 85, 86

RICHARDSON, Nancy, 40
RICHARDSON, Thomas, 5, 17, 21, 35
RICHARDSON, Thomas R., 21
RICHARDSON, William, 5, 21, 35, 49
RICHMOND, David, 41
RICKERING, Samuel, 57
RICKETT, John, 8
RIDGELY, Charles, 55, 56, 57, 58
RINEHARD, John, 18, 67
RINEHARD, Rosanna, 67
RINHARD, John, 67
RINHARD, Rosanna, 67
ROBBINS, Silas W., 45
ROBERTS, Samuel M., 35
ROBERTSON, John, 61, 63
ROBINSON, 28
ROBINSON, David, 2, 4
ROBINSON, James, 50, 80
ROBINSON, John, 4, 13, 14, 16, 65, 85
RODGERS, Charles, 84
RODGERS, George, 28
ROGERS, Phillip, 41, 61
ROSE, Denison, 16, 45
ROSE, Dennison, 11, 15, 35
ROSE, Ezekiel, 3
ROSE, Joseph H., 6
ROSE, Susan, 6
ROSS, Elizabeth, 49, 58
ROSS, Griffith, 49
ROSS, James, 49, 58, 60
ROWLAND, David, 44
RUDISILL, Jacob, 2
RUST, James B., 79
SAFFARRAN, George, 79
SAUNDERSON, John, 53
SAWYER, Andrew, 1, 2, 30,

SAWYER, Andrew (Cont.) 31, 34, 37, 39, 40
SAWYER, Archer, 65
SAWYER, George, 23, 30, 33, 37, 39, 40, 41, 60, 77
SAWYER, Harvey, 24
SAWYER, James, 23
SAWYER, Mathew, 8, 9, 23, 65
SAWYER, Rachael, 30, 33
SAWYER, Sampson, 5, 8, 9, 10, 20, 24, 30, 31, 33, 35, 37, 39, 47, 48, 60, 76, 77, 85
SAWYER, Thomas, 35
SAWYER, William, 33
SAWYER JR., Andrew, 23
SAWYERS, Sampson, 25
SCHOTT, Charles Frederick Albert, 61
SCHOTT, Charles Fredrick Albert, 63, 64
SCOTT, 80
SCOTT, Andrew, 18
SCOTT, Andrew M., 70, 74
SCOTT, I., 41
SCOTT, Rachel, 74
SCOTT, Rachel C., 74
SCOTT, Richard M., 4
SCOTT, William, 23, 28, 32, 33, 47, 53, 59, 69, 73, 75, 77
SELDEN, William, 26, 28
SHARKY, James, 73
SHAVER, Christopher, 15, 16
SHAVER, Jacob, 67
SHAVER, Mary, 16
SHAWER, John, 49
SHIELDS, William H., 62, 63, 64

SHIRKEY, John, 70
SHOEMAKER, 36
SHOEMAKER, William, 36
SHOVERS, Boston, 45
SHUMATE, John, 52
SHUMDLE, John, 75
SIBERT, Abraham, 41
SIBERT, Jane, 41
SILLINGTON, A., 84
SILLINGTON, Alexander, 43
SILLINGTON, Andrew, 43
SILLINGTON, Ann B., 43
SILLINGTON, John M. D., 43
SILLINGTON, Mary J., 43
SILLINGTON, Rebecca, 43
SILLINGTON, William, 43
SIMMONS, E., 13
SIMMONS, Ephraim, 13, 80
SIMMONS, Ruth, 80
SIMPSON, James, 58
SISSON, Abner, 15
SISSON, Ann, 15
SISSON, Armistead, 15
SISSON, Becky, 15
SIVELY, 11
SIVELY, George, 10, 14, 31, 34, 40, 47, 51, 54, 58, 59, 66, 69, 70, 75, 76, 78, 85
SIVELY, Johathan, 54
SIVELY, Jonathan, 54, 75
SIVELY, Mary, 75
SIZER, Daniel, 15
SIZER, Sarah, 15
SKEEN, Robert, 50, 51, 64, 80
SKEENE, Johnathan, 10
SKIDMORE, Levi, 84
SLOWN, John, 39, 43
SMITH, 19
SMITH, Archibald, 47
SMITH, Henry, 18, 19, 33, 34, 36, 37, 66, 67
SMITH, Meshach, 15
SMITH, Peter, 52
SMITH, Preston, 54
SMITH, Rebecca, 15
SMITH, Richard, 6, 7, 18, 20, 29, 43, 65, 71, 73
SMITH, William, 10, 44, 48, 51, 59, 80
SNEAD, 84
SNEAD, Ann, 84
SNEAD, Judith, 3
SNEAD, Nancy, 83
SNEAD, Richard, 83, 84
SNEAD, William, 3, 19, 41, 44, 48, 51, 59
SOLOM, Jacob, 65
SOUTHLAND, Vincent, 41
SOWERS, John C., 40
SPOTTS, William, 32
SPROWL, 2
SPROWL, John, 72
STATON, James, 79
STEEL, Daniel, 67
STEEL, Elizabeth, 38
STEEL, George, 36
STEEL, I., 40, 53, 59
STEEL, Isaac, 2, 6, 7, 30, 31, 35-37, 40, 44, 53, 59, 64, 68, 70, 72, 74-76, 79, 80, 82
STEEL, James, 38
STEEL, John, 67
STEEL, Julia, 35, 36, 70
STEEL, Rachel, 67
STEELE, Benjamin F., 28
STEELE, Isaac, 23, 24
STEPHEN, Robert, 36
STEVENS, Benjamin, 62
STILL, Bartlette, 54

STILLINGS, Jane, 44, 50, 51
STILLINGS, Joseph, 32, 38, 44, 45, 50, 51
STILLINGS, Joseph B., 73
STILLWELL, Steven, 4
STONE, John, 8, 85
STOVER, Daniel, 75
STUART, Lewis, 14, 69
STULL, George, 5, 44, 45
STULL, Jacob, 45
STULL, Jane, 44, 45
STULL, John, 44, 45
STULL SR., George, 45
SUBLETT, Samuel, 53
SUSBER, George, 66
SWAN, James, 61, 62
SWANN, David Cooper, 61, 63
SWANN, James, 61, 62, 63
SWEENEY, Benjamin, 75
SWEETLAND, E., 44
SYBERT, Abraham, 60
TACHETT, J. H., 7
TACKITT, Ann, 17
TACKITT, Nimrod, 17
TATE, Comfort, 47, 61, 71
TATE, David, 47, 61, 71
TAYLOR, 11
TAYLOR, Amanda, 52
TAYLOR, Charles T., 84
TAYLOR, George, 4
TAYLOR, H. P., 35, 44
TAYLOR, Hugh, 36, 44
TAYLOR, Hugh P., 35, 44, 51, 52, 69
TAYLOR, Iven P., 4
TAYLOR, John, 24, 46, 51, 52
TAYLOR, Mary Ann C., 52
TAYLOR, Sally, 51, 52

TAYLOR, Sarah A. E. A. F., 84
TAYLOR, Watkins, 52
TAYLOR, William, 11, 52
TAYLOR, William B., 7, 8
TERRILL, Elizabeth, 75
TERRILL, James, 59
TERRILL, William, 29, 30, 40, 47, 50, 52-55, 65, 66, 80, 85, 86
TERRILL, William A., 47, 58
TERRILL, William H., 17, 23, 29-34, 37, 39, 40, 45, 47, 49, 50, 52-55, 58, 64, 69, 70, 75, 77, 80
TERRY, William, 9
THOMAS, Benjamin, 85
THOMAS, James, 85
THOMAS, Richard, 10
THOMAS, Robert, 33
THOMAS JR., John, 35
THOMPSON, Benjamin, 37, 83, 84
THOMPSON, Elizabeth, 28, 84
THOMPSON, William P., 54
THOMSON, Benjamin, 84
TILGHMAN, William, 58
TINSLEY, Bennet, 77
TOLBERT, Charles, 3, 20, 71
TRAVERS, Andrew, 23
TRESSLER, Henry, 6, 25, 46, 59
TRESSLER, Jacob, 10, 25
TURNER, Fittieus, 69
TURNER, Fittius, 59, 67, 75, 76, 82, 83, 86
VANCLEVE JR., Aaron, 62
VANLEAR, John A., 17
VANSTAVERN, Agnes, 48

VANSTAVERN, C., 38, 74
VANSTAVERN, Cornelius, 19, 34, 41, 43, 44, 48, 51, 59
VANSTAVERN, Nicholas, 19, 35, 36
VANSTAVERN, William, 19
VINCENT, John, 74
VINCENT, Michael, 37, 40, 41, 74
VOYERS, Robert, 21
WALDERMAN, Francis, 61, 63, 64
WALKER, John, 39
WALTON, Edmund P., 51
WALTS, James, 11
WANSTRUF, Catherine, 18, 19
WANSTRUF, Jacob, 18, 19
WARD, William, 84
WARDER, Jeremiah, 56
WARDES, Jeremiah, 58
WARWICK, Andrew, 84
WATKINS, 75
WAYT, George, 50, 66
WAYT, John, 40
WAYT, Kesiah, 50
WAYT, Mary, 66
WEAS, George, 45
WEBB, Lewis, 53
WEEKS, George, 38
WETSON, Dorsey, 20
WETSON, Elizabeth, 20
WETSON, Franklin, 20
WETSON, Henry, 20
WETSON, Pulina, 20
WETSON, Vauen, 20
WHITE, James, 81
WHITE, Lucy, 78, 81
WHITE, Robert, 56
WHITE, T., 25

WHITE, Thomas, 25, 78, 81
WHITE, Thomas T., 24, 25, 78, 81
WHITLOCKE, J. B., 54
WILLIAMS, Alice G., 53
WILLIAMS, Elisha, 10, 31, 52, 59
WILLIAMS, Elisha B., 18
WILLIAMS, Hazel, 10, 30, 31, 38, 43, 51, 53
WILLIAMS, John, 69
WILLIAMS, John G., 53
WILLIAMS, Margaret, 59
WILLIAMS, Nancy, 30, 31, 43, 51
WILLIAMS, William C., 53
WILSON, Alexander, 36
WILSON, Elizabeth, 3, 6, 7, 25, 46
WILSON, I., 22
WILSON, J., 7
WILSON, Mathew, 3, 6, 25, 46
WILSON, Rebecca, 36, 44, 67
WILSON, T., 7
WILSON, William, 70
WINCHESTER, David, 57
WINTZ, Richard H., 85
WITHERS, Polly, 15
WITHROW, James, 15
WOLF, Abraham, 9, 75
WOLF, Isaac, 9, 32
WOLF, Jacob, 9, 13, 21, 32, 42, 75, 80, 81
WOLF, John, 9, 75
WOLF, Magdalene, 9, 75
WOLF, Mary, 42
WOLF, Mary Elizabeth, 75
WOLF JR., Abraham, 75
WOMACK, William, 15

WOOD, 29
WOOD, Joshua, 75
WOOD, Mary, 75
WOODSON, Tschar, 53
WOODVILLE, James, 2
WRIGHT, Catherine, 28, 79
WRIGHT, Cathy, 29
WRIGHT, James, 50
WRIGHT, John, 28, 29, 79, 80
WRIGHT, Peter, 3, 4, 6-8, 20, 22, 43, 59, 71, 73
WRIGHT, William, 9
YOUNG, Robert, 62
YOUNG, William, 70

www.ingramcontent.com/pod-product-compliance
Lightning Source LLC
Chambersburg PA
CBHW060412090426
42734CB00011B/2293